Madison Clinton Peters

Sanctified Spice

Pungent Seasonings from the Pulpit

Madison Clinton Peters

Sanctified Spice
Pungent Seasonings from the Pulpit

ISBN/EAN: 9783337417581

Printed in Europe, USA, Canada, Australia, Japan

Cover: Foto ©Lupo / pixelio.de

More available books at **www.hansebooks.com**

SANCTIFIED SPICE

OR

PUNGENT SEASONINGS FROM THE PULPIT

BY

MADISON C. PETERS

PASTOR OF BLOOMINGDALE REFORMED CHURCH, NEW YORK CITY
AND AUTHOR OF "EMPTY PEWS," "THE PATH OF GLORY,"
"POPULAR SINS," ETC., ETC.

✚

"AND SOME OF THE SONS OF THE PRIESTS MADE
THE OINTMENT OF THE SPICES."—I. CHRON., 9 : 30

❖

NEW YORK
WILBUR B. KETCHAM
2 COOPER UNION

TO MY DEAR WIFE
WHOSE CHEERFULNESS IS AN INSPIRATION
I LOVINGLY DEDICATE THESE WORDS

PREFACE.

EDWARD IRVING published four discourses under the title of "Orations," giving as the reason that the very word "sermon" was indicative of dullness. We send forth these homely selections from our sermons, preludes, and Friday night talks under the title of "Sanctified Spice," because we believe that brightness, sarcasm and wit have a rightful place in the pulpit. Short sermons are insisted on by the taste of the day. Why this impatience of preaching? Is it not because sermons lack the things that glow, brighten, convince, subdue—"thoughts that breathe and words that burn"?

There may be some things in these pages that will cause you to smile. I have yet to learn that it is a greater sin to smile than to sleep in church, or that sinners will be attracted if the countenance be somber and the voice sepulchral. When we stand up in the pulpit we too often change our voices, and drone, cant, moan, croak and funeralize religion with a countenance grave enough to break an undertaker's heart.

That these words may further the cause of common sense, truth, righteousness, temperance, humanity, and of Christ, is the hope and the prayer of

THE AUTHOR.

BLOOMINGDALE CHURCH STUDY,
    New York City.

CONTENTS.

vii

CONTENTS.

I.

WHILE I have broken away from slavery
to ecclesiastical traditions and customs, let it
be distinctly understood that I am trying to
build up here a distinctively *Christian* church.
These consecrated walls shall resound only
with evangelical truth. This holy place will
be the witness only of worship that is pure
and of doctrine that is sound. My theology
is spelled in six letters, C-h-r-i-s-t, Christ, but
not Christ as the center of a mere theology,
or the patron of an ecclesiasticism. The world
is sick and tired of dry, withered, juiceless
theological terms and phrases. It cares not
for, nor understands, terminology and vocabulary. We preach Christ as the redemption
from sin; Christ as the brother of man; Christ
as the treasury of riches for the poor; Christ
as the shop of soul-medicines for the sick;
Christ as the solace for the afflicted; Christ as
the hope in every discouragement; Christ as
the guide in every perplexity; Christ as the

reform for every wrong; Christ as the protection of the persecuted; Christ as the recovery for the deserted; Christ as the beauty for the young; Christ as the wisdom of the aged; Christ, while we live, the rule for our conversation; when we die, Christ the hope of our glorification.

Many men who make loud noise in the world about their orthodoxy, instead of preaching the Gospel of Christ expound the systematic theology *inferred* from the Gospel through the epistles of Paul. He who reads Paul often reads mystery. The words of Christ are simple and easily understood. Paul in mind, heart and will was the grandest man that ever trod the earth since first the Almighty sent it circling round the sun, and he wrote as he was moved by the Holy Ghost; but Jesus Christ is a Saviour, whose utterances were the statements of the Divine Consciousness itself. The rule of my preaching is the preaching of the Gospel with the gospels. The world is hungering and thirsting for less theology and more Christianity, less of Paul and more of Christ. There are plenty of sermons on justification, verbal inspiration, effectual calling, and the efficacy of the sacraments. But the Sermon on the Mount is seldom preached, and all that Christianity is meant

to do in making the life pure is left undone.
Our duty is no longer to be honest and true
and self-denying and pure, like the Divine
Pattern, but to hold accurately the creed of
the church.

Not without cause does the Scotch believer
cry :

" There's nae gospel noo, lassie,
    There's nae covenant blood;
There's nae altar noo, lassie,
    There's nae Lamb o' God.

" There's nae Chalmers noo, lassie,
    There's nae gude McCheyne;
And the dear, dear Cross they preached, lassie,
    The dear, dear Cross is gane.

" Folks dinna want the Cross, lassie,
    They've cutten down the tree;
And naebody believes in it
    But fules like you and me."

II.

WHAT IS IT TO BE A CHRISTIAN?

BAPTISMS, confirmations and church-memberships do not make Christians. You cannot make Christians to order by law any more than you can make Americans out of foreigners by the mere act of naturalization. He is an American, no matter where born, who has an American heart, whose sympathies and choices, labors and sacrifices, make him deserve the proud name of American. So the mere act of baptism or church-membership gives a man a poor title to the Christian name. Paul said that the man was not a Jew who was one outwardly, that the mere rite of circumcision was nothing; that he only was a Jew who was one inwardly, at heart.

The Christian Church differs from the Jewish Church mainly in caring less for things ceremonial and more for things spiritual, less for rites and more for righteousness.

It is very important to understand and believe the truth which relates to Christ and his

kingdom; but the most unhesitating assent of
the intellect to all the creeds, catechisms, commentaries and systems framed in eighteen
hundred years will make no man a Christian.
Instead of making more noise in the world
about our orthodoxy than the Master ever did,
and making such elaborate and ostentatious
prayers as to be troublesome to our neighbor,
let us do justly, love mercy, and walk humbly
with our God. He is the Christian who prac-
tically follows him " who went about doing
good," and not he who is loaded and clogged
with the mere theories of dead men on the
subject, that leave no scope for anything else.

> " 'Tis not the wide phylactery,
>   Nor stubborn fasts, nor stated prayers,
> That make us saints; we judge the tree
>   By what it bears.

> " And when a man can live apart
>   From works, on theologic trust,
> I know the blood about his heart
>   Is dry as dust."

A man may be a life-long member of the most
orthodox church in Christendom, and never
miss a communion or a prayer-meeting, if he
is mean, selfish and careless of the world's condition, he is no Christian; while on the other
hand a man may not be a communicant, and
even not much of a church-goer, and yet if he

spends his whole life for others he is so much like Christ I shall call him a Christian. I do not depreciate a public profession of Christ in the ordinary church modes, but I believe that the grandest profession of the religion of Christ is that Christ-like, self-denying charity which finds its chief pleasure in ministering to the woes and brightening the lives of our fellow-men.

These lines describe the feelings and actions of a Christian:

"Blest is the man whose softening heart
    Feels all another's pain;
To whom the supplicating eye
    Was never raised in vain;

"Whose breast expands with generous warmth,
    A stranger's woes to feel,
And bleeds in pity o'er the wound
    He wants the power to heal.

"To gentle offices of love
    His feet are never slow;
He views, through mercy's melting eye,
    A brother in a foe."

III.

HAVE you not had your admiration excited by hearing it said of any one, " She is a useful woman"? Would that I could inspire you with an abhorrence of being useless and an ambition to be useful. Shrivel not into a despicable selfishness, cherish a yearning after benevolent activity, and feel as if it were but half living to live only for yourselves.

> "O woman, forget not thou, earth's honored priest,
>   Its tongue, its soul, its life, its pulse, its heart,
>   In earth's great chorus to sustain thy part!
>   Chiefest of guests at love's ungrudging feast,
>   Play not the niggard; spurn thy native clod,
>   And *self* disown:
>   Live unto thy neighbor, live unto thy God,
>   Not unto thyself alone."

Woman's heart is supposed to be the very dwelling-place of mercy, and a useless and selfish woman is a libel upon her sex. We call upon you to be our sisters of charity, to go forth on errands of mercy to the abodes of sickness and poverty without abjuring all pretensions to the character of wifehood and motherhood. Loathe that spurious sentimentality which weeps over the imaginary woes of a novel, but turns away with a callous heart from those real sufferings which abound on every hand. You do most for yourselves when you do most for others. It is not enough that you pity the sorrows of the poor and the suffering; what your heart pities your hands must do; what you pray for you must strive to attain.

If you have a desire to live in the true sense of the word, you can least afford to be useless. It is lamentable to see how many women live only as a waste and weight on fast-flying time. O you poor souls living in uselessness, how can I make you see what you are losing! What can I say but

"Rise up, ye women that are at ease,
  Tremble, ye careless daughters,"

and repeat the old call, " Awake, ye that sleep, and arise from the dead, and Christ shall give you light."

In the woman form of merciful ministry humanity feels the touch as of an angel from heaven. Say not the doors of useful service are closed against you when there are so many poor to help, so many sick longing for the sound of a woman's voice and the touch of a woman's hand. If you have an earnest purpose, it will not want for a sphere, it will make its own sphere. Would you realize the divinest of womanhood's ideals and be "as the angels," listen to the moans of suffering around you. Hearken to the voice that whispers in your soul; begin with some plain, practical, petty duty immediately at hand, and in faithfulness to the lowly duty your life will gradually be brought under the power of a supreme purpose,

> "And so make life, death, and that fast forever,
> One grand, sweet song."

If you should die to-day, could friends look upon your quiet face and feel that death had bereft them of a benefactor? Could they lay snow-white flowers against your hair and smooth it down with tearful tenderness and fold your hands with lingering caress? If you should die to-day, could woe-worn humanity call to mind with loving thought some kindly deed the icy hand had wrought, some gentle word the frozen lips had said, errands on which willing feet had sped? Would you be mourned? A dry-eyed funeral is a sad sight. Be always sure of being useful. This will make your life comfortable, your death happy, your funeral sad, your account glorious, and your eternity blessed. And remember,

"It isn't the thing you do, dear,
  It's the thing you leave undone,
Which gives you a bit of heartache
  At the setting of the sun.
The tender word forgotten,
  The letter you did not write,
The flower you might have sent, dear,
  Are your haunting ghosts to-night.

"The stone you might have lifted
  Out of a brother's way,
The bit of heartsome counsel
  You were hurried too much to say,
The loving touch of the hand, dear,
  The gentle and winsome tone
That you had no time nor thought for,
  With troubles enough of your own.

"The little acts of kindness,
  So easily out of mind;
Those chances to be angels,
  Which every one may find;
They come in night and silence,
  Each chill, reproachful wraith,
When hope is faint and flagging,
  And a blight has dropped on faith.

"For life is all too short, dear,
  And sorrow is all too great,
To suffer our slow compassion
  That tarries until too late;
And it's not the thing you do, dear,
  It's the thing you leave undone,
Which gives you the bit of heartache
  At the setting of the sun."

IV.

No life can be lifted above stale mediocrity without the inward glow and divine passion called enthusiasm. Kindled from truth and eternal principles, it is "God in us." Emerson truly says that "every great and commanding movement in the annals of the world is the triumph of enthusiasm." Lord Lytton says, "Enthusiasm is the genius of sincerity, and truth accomplishes no victories without it." Enthusiasm gives a man irresistible power. What power Christians would be in the world if each one could honestly say with Brainerd, "Oh, that I were a flaming fire in the hands of my God!" We need at this time what the Chinese convert told the missionary his people wanted, "men with hot hearts to tell us of the love of Christ." Do you find in this world lukewarmness in any one department of real life? Do you find anything like apathy when men believe their interests or safety are involved? It is only skepticism that suffers enthusiasm in the things of Cæsar and will not endure enthusiasm in the more important things of God. We profess to believe that the world of sinners outside of Christ will be eternally lost unless turned from their evil ways; and yet we so live by our indifference as to give the lie to such profession, or else stamp ourselves without the commonest feeling of humanity. It is impossible to believe the truths of the Gospel and yet be apathetic. I do not believe in religious excitement, but I do believe in excitement in religion. The cross is the most restless and resistless of agitators, and if your religion does not excite you, it is because you have no religion. If you believe the tear-compelling story of Jesus and his love, the best feelings and sympathies of your nature will be roused to their highest pitch, and you will love with an enthusiastic love, and praise with intense gratitude him who so loved and bled and died for us. If you feel no quenchless love, fiery zeal, and glowing enthusiasm for Christ's glory, you may disguise it as you like, but indeed and in truth you do not believe that Christ died that sinners might be redeemed; or you believe in Calvary just as you believe in Gettysburg; you believe in Jesus Christ as you believe in Washington, or in some dead

fact which belongs to history and has no living connection with you or bearing on your
destiny. We hear much about the triumphant march of the Roman Catholic Church.
To what is the Roman Church indebted for its
triumph? To the indifference of Protestants
and the enthusiasm of Catholics. It is because the Catholics are thoroughly devoted
and in earnest, and are prepared to suffer in
order to support what they believe to be true.
If you believe the Gospel, you must be in-
fluenced by it. If twelve million Romans
sacrificed their lives to gratify the ambition
of Cæsar; if four million Frenchmen laid
down their lives in the war-path cut by Napoleon through Europe and whitened foreign
shores with their bones—soldiers of Christ, are
you not willing to sacrifice worldly ambition,
to sacrifice all for Christ? God grant it!

V.

THE CHURCH AND THE STAGE.

THE theater owns its origin to religion. In Greece, India, and China the drama was originally a religious ceremony, and it was intended to promote religion. In the course of time the drama ceased to be a religious ceremony and became a work of art.

Every student of church history knows that the modern drama sprang originally from the church. In the dark ages the priests put the whole of theology on the stage, and in this way the rude and unlettered mob that gathered on saints' days were taught in an effective way the truths of religion, so that in the Christian era the first theaters were the churches and the first actors the priests.

But secular competition grew apace, and in 1378 the Dean and Chapter of St. Paul's Cathedral petitioned Richard III. to stop certain dramatic performances which were being gotten up in London outside the church. Why? Because the cathedral clergy of St.

Paul's had spent so much money on church scenery and costumes inside the cathedral, they were eager to crush all secular competition.

In Elizabeth's reign the secular drama had grown so popular that a preacher exclaims, "Woe is me! At the play-house it is not possible to get a seat, while at the church vacant seats are plenty." The clergy did not object to the principle of acting, or because the play was immoral, except when it satirized the drunken and smoking rector. Nor did the clergy object to the play because it hurt the people, but because it pleased them. They groaned when the people shouted.

God has implanted a dramatic element in most of our natures; recognized and cultivated it in the Bible. It is not something built up outside of ourselves by Thespis and Æschylus and Sophocles and Euripides and Terence and Plautus and Seneca and Congreve and Farquhar and Corneille and Alfieri and Goldsmith and Sheridan and Shakespeare. Man is not responsible for the dramatic element in his soul, but for the perversion of it.

If vacant seats are so plenty in the church, whose fault is it? The human mind is the same in the pew as in the theater. The world suffers more from too little dramatic power

in the church than from too much outside of
it. A preacher asked Garrick, the tragedian,
"Why is it you are able to produce so much
more effect with the recital of your fictions
than we do by the delivery of the most important truths?" "My lord," said Garrick,
"you speak truths as if they were fictions;
we speak fictions as if they were truths." And
wherever to-day, all Christendom through,
there is a man with graceful gestures, modu-
lated voice, elegant expression, appropriate
emotion, and graceful action; wherever you
find a man as natural and impressive, as audi-
ble and as interesting as the actor, you will
find a full church. Let the preachers work at
the people with the same power, intelligence,
and will as the actor is obliged to work at the
public, depend upon it their achievements will
be in proportion. The actor does not grumble
because the people won't come to the theater.
He says, "I am to blame." People don't come
to church because they are not interested.
Let us learn from the actor how to read and
how to infuse life into our service.

Other things besides religion are good.
Dickens' works are eternal arguments against
injustice, and in writing novels he was as well
employed as in preaching the Gospel. Mendels-
sohn, by his sublime compositions, did better

serve the world than going out as a missionary
to China; and Shakespeare served the world
and his Maker better as a dramatist than as a
bishop preaching sermons that nobody wanted
to hear. The arts and sciences must go hand
in hand with religion and morality.

The church of the past stood aloof from the
world. The church of the future will assimilate with it. The church has spent much time
peering into amusements to see what evil they
contained, and has kept digging away at this
instead of putting divine grace into them and
letting that elevate and regulate them. We
have been absorbed in ferreting out and de-
claiming against the evil, and forgotten that
we have a corresponding duty to develop the
good. The church has failed to regulate
popular amusements, it has withdrawn itself
from them, and if the devil has come in and
taken full possession the church is to blame.

I know that I overstep the mark of received
church opinion, but I would rather be right
than consistent. If the church has, with mistaken zeal, fostered a false position, it would
be cowardly, having discovered the error, to
withhold the truth from society through fear of
being turned on and called inconsistent. This
age needs men who have the courage to meet
prejudice. Let us bring the leaven of the

Gospel into the amusement lump, and teach the people how to use amusements without abusing them, and save the church from her present humiliating attitude as the declared enemy of the drama, from attending which she has no power to restrain her members. The world is growing better; the church is growing wiser. We are in a transition age. Religious opinion is bridging over the scandalous chasm which has so long existed between church and stage. As an ethical question, most persons are agreed that amusements in the abstract are not wrong. Some people mistake their prejudices for conscientious scruples. "Man has an animal nature as well as rational faculties; he has instincts that are purely animal as well as characteristics purely intellectual and spiritual, and the playing out of these impulses within the limits of moderation are just as sinless as in the animal pure and simple." The mind kept on the continual stretch of serious duty will prematurely lose its healthy action. Old and young alike must have their times of sport, and it is not necessary that we bring the hours of recreation under too rigid scrutiny of reason. The scrutiny of *conscience* must be there. However pleasant it may be to do wrong, it is never right to do it, and sin committed in the pursuit of pleasure is as sinful as if done for the sake of profit. But having made this reservation, the wisest of us can sometimes afford to lay aside our dignity and become children. As Martin Luther romped with the children, and the immortal Chalmers trundled a hoop, so our amusements, trifling in themselves, may be considered wise for the same reason "that the bow needs to be completely unbent." I do not take the untenable and unchristian position of condemning everything in life unless invested with seriousness. That would make life too gloomy. But if, on the other hand, we make life all sunshine, and sport continually in its beams, like insects of the day, pleasure-seekers only, it is a very different thing. That which may be commended as an occasional recreation becomes very unmanly or unwomanly if made the object of daily pursuit. Our amusements may be prostituted to evil; so may horses. Because they are often the gambler's richest resources shall we refuse to use them? The theater is primarily for amusement, and not for moral instruction. The home, the social circle, the church, the Sunday-school, the companionship of good books, and, above all, the Bible, are to teach us what is right and true.

The charge that religion is scoffed at on the

stage is false. Hypocrites and charlatans occasionally furnish subjects for its characterization. The cause of religion does not suffer when its spurious representatives are held up to ridicule and contempt. Christ did the same thing. The closing passage of an old play ("The Hypocrite") containing such a character would seem to be a sufficient answer to the charge to which I have just alluded:

"Nay, now, my dear sir, I must take the liberty to tell you, you carry things too far and go from one extreme to another. What! Because a worthless wretch has imposed upon you under the fallacious show of an austere grimace, will you needs have it that everybody is like him? Confound the good with the bad, and conclude there are no truly religious in the world? Leave, my dear sir, such rash conclusions to fools and libertines. Let us be careful to distinguish as between virtue and the appearance of it. Guard, if possible, against doing honor to hypocrisy; but at the same time allow there is no character in life greater or more valuable than that of the truly devout, nor anything more noble or more beautiful than the fervor of a sincere piety."

All actors are not moral. All preachers are not moral. There are bad men in all professions. There are men and women on the stage whose characters are as spotless and their lives as beneficient as any in our churches. Crimes are committed on the stage; so they are in the Bible. Goodness and badness are put in opposition in both books and plays. The chief themes of the theater are the passions of men. So are the subjects for the chisel of Angelo, the brush of Guido, the pencil of Doré, the burden of the Sermon on the Mount by Christ, in whose lips there was no guile, and whose every thought was without spot or blemish. If the exposure of sin is an indecency, to be consistent all the literature of the world, both sacred and profane, must be committed to the flames. Call the roll of all the plays that achieve the widest and most permanent success. They are as innocent as milk, and the leaders of the stage would be astonished at being accused of producing an immoral piece. The preacher contrasts virtue and vice from a positive point of view; the dramatist presents pictorially the contrasts between virtue and vice, and I know of no standard play in which the former is not always triumphant in the end. The Roman actor charged with having corrupted the youth of the city said before the Senate:

> "When do we bring a vice upon the stage
> That goes off unpunished? Do we teach
> By the success of wicked undertakings
> Others to tread in their forbidden steps?
> We show no arts of Lydian panderism,
> Corinthian poisons, Persian flatteries,
> But mulcted so in the conclusion that
> Even those spectators that were so inclined
> Go home changed men."

The true end of the drama is to represent human nature; to teach a complete knowledge of human character. Give a man all kinds of knowledge in history, poetry, philosophy, science, languages; let him possess the graces and bearing of a god, and the golden thoughts and musical words of a poet—without a knowledge of human nature all his other accomplishments would hurl him into an absurdity. "Know thyself" was a maxim of old Greek philosophy. Know thyself and all thy fellow-creatures is the truer and wiser maxim of a higher philosophy. In the writings of the great dramatist we have the following types of character depicted in the following personages: in Marcus Brutus, a self-sacrificing patriot; in Macbeth, a brave soldier corrupted by ambition; in Othello, a guileless nature ruined by jealousy; in King Lear, a hot-blooded tyrant thwarted into madness; in Shylock, a revengeful man carried away by his passion; in King John, a thorough-going villain; in Richard III., a spoiled child, angry and tearful by turns, blaming everybody but himself for his misfortunes; in Benedict, a smart fellow who finds it easier to live at other people's expense; in Henry V., an accomplished king; in Prospero, the portrait of a Christian philosopher.

These grand plays, to which every element of my nature responds, interpreted by good histrionic talent, with all the adjuncts of scenery and costume, are to me sources of rich pleasure and intellectual improvement.

Water cannot rise higher than its source, and the character of the theater cannot be sustained above the character of those who attend it. Playwrights and actors are not to blame for what we often get on the stage. The Americans like slang and vulgarity. Playwrights and actors do not live to write and act; they have the bread-and-butter human weakness, and write and act to live. They know what the people want, and they give it to them. The noble sentiment raises feeble applause, but the word that looks two ways, or the exhibition of doubtful propriety, brings all the feet down and makes all hands clap. The theater and opera will never in tone and tendency be above the life that attends them. The demand will control the supply. In nothing else do Americans show so much bad taste as in their indorsement of plays and players. "Hamlet," "Macbeth," "King Lear," or "Richard III"—are these the types which most frequently appear? Look at the placards on the walls for the answer. And the Shakespeares, Goldsmiths and Sheridans

are not likely to be popular so long as people
throng the theaters to hear poor puns and
silly songs which the compounders of gayety
burlesque provide.

Still I am hopeful for the future. A larger
and more refined class of people attend the
theater now than ever. A higher tone of
morals prevails in the best plays and is manifested in the character of the players.

The church has made a tremendous mistake
in its wholesale denunciation of the theater.
A larger part of the community attend the
theater, and the majority of our population
are moral and virtuous. Amusements are
proper for Christians because they are right,
and they are right because the divine law
written in our hearts makes them so. There
is nothing in the precepts of our religion that
makes us march down the path of life to the
tune of the "Dead March in Saul." The pulpit's vituperation of the theatrical profession is
so unchristian as only a clergyman who never
saw a good play would ever dream of making.
The stage seldom or never strikes back. The
numerous scandals of American clergymen
now serving terms in the various penitentia-
ries of the land afford legitimate material for
the stage. These materials remain unused
because the dramatist, the manager, and the

actor have too great a respect for the religion of Christ to weaken it by emphasizing the sins of any of his servants. Some men who write against the sensuality of the stage remind me of the preacher in Canada who declaimed against dancing in such a manner that the dancing went on but the parson was himself discharged on account of the vulgarity of his discourse. The time has passed for offensive dictation and inquisitorial condemnation on the part of bigots.

The theater is here to stay. Reform is the note of the future. Eliminate the bad. Encourage the good. The shameful posters, the female attire, or rather the lack of it, the compromising attitudes, the silly things accepted, the commonplace persons admired and commended—thunder as much at these as you will. Let ridicule, sarcasm, and denunciation exhaust their armories upon these abuses, these positive evils.

"Can I go to the theater?" asks the Christian. I answer, If you *can*. "Let every man be persuaded in his own mind." Refuse to do or go where your conscience forbids, but refrain also from condemning your neighbor, whose conscience may not require him to walk in the same path you have marked out for yourself.

From amusements that demand of you an outlay beyond your means you had better stand aloof. If you have dollars and days for the theater, and mites and minutes for the church, you need reconstruction. Confirmed theater-goers are unfitted for life's duties. I have scores of women in my church who pay good prices for their matinee seats Saturday afternoons who reluctantly drop a dime in the contribution-box on Sunday. These women never have time nor money for the Lord's work. How many of you are so given to levity, so giddy, so frivolous, that you are incapable of a serious thought! Your hearts are set on having "a good time."

Once a man stood stunned at the first sight of the Niagara. When he got his breath back he simply and coolly said, "I wonder how much machinery all this would turn?" We are told there is enough power there when converted into electricity to lighten the world. And there is enough vigorous manhood and womanhood in this city, if rightly applied, to illumine our whole country. But behold the thousands wasting that power, throwing it to the four winds!

Dugald Stewart tells of a man who spent fifteen years trying to balance a broom on his chin. Hundreds of men and women in New

York are scarcely better employed. Their lives are summed up in rising, dressing, dining, wining, loafing, visiting, pleasure-seeking, and sleeping. Busy men about trifles, pitiful butterfly species, flitting from flower to flower, and dying like autumnal insects, despised and forgotten.

Charles Lamb once wrote a play for the stage, and he went to see it enacted. The play was condemned, and loudest hissing came from the gallery where Charles Lamb sat, and the audience looked and saw that it was the author of the play who was hissing his own production.

If at last we are compelled to look back upon a wasted life, we ourselves will be the severest critics. And remember this: when you go out of this world and your life has been wasted, no *encore* can ever bring you back to reënact it. "As the tree falleth so it lieth." Your character at the last moment will be your character through all eternity. Mr. Palmer, the London actor, dropped dead on the stage while quoting the words of the play, "O God, is there another and a better world?" I do not know what will be your exit, but in that hour there will come before you all you have been and all you might have been. O men and women of the theatrical profession to whom these words may come, prepare for the closing scenes of this life, when the footlights will be the burning world, the orchestra the resurrection trumpets, the tragedy the upheaval of a world of graves, and the closing scene the dispersing of the audience to their everlasting homes of gladness or sorrow.

Amid all his levity and excess, Burns had moments of deep seriousness, recognized man's spiritual and immortal part, and the necessity of living for something higher than this present world. I was struck the other day with these lines, a grand sermon, which he sent to an intimate friend:

> "The voice of Nature loudly cries—
> And many a message from the skies—
> That something in us never dies;
> That on this frail, uncertain state
> Hang matters of eternal weight;
> That future life in worlds unknown
> Must take its hue from this alone,
> Whether as heavenly glory bright,
> Or dark as misery's woeful night.
> Since, then, my honored first of friends,
> On this poor being all depends,
> Let us the important NOW employ,
> And live as those who never die."

VI.

SPIRITUALISM in America was born in 1848 in Hydesville, Wayne County, N. Y. The house of John D. Fox was disturbed by noises which were at first attributed to rats and mice, but which were soon recognized as rappings, made seemingly by invisible knuckles. One night the rappings commenced with unusual violence. Mr. Fox tried the window-sashes to see if they rattled in the wind, and found them all secure; but Kate, his twelve-year-old daughter, observed that when he shook the sashes the rappings followed; and turning in the direction from which the sound proceeded, and snapping her fingers she exclaimed, "Here, Old Splitfoot, do as I do."

The knockings which instantly followed so frightened Kate and her sister Margaret that they for a time had no wish to further cultivate the acquaintance of "Old Splitfoot." The mother, however, carried on the conversation, and received a message which professed to come from the spirit of Charles B. Rosma, who said he had been murdered in that house some years ago. Then there was a general rumpus; the tables tipped, the bedsteads raised, and the chairs upset, until it seemed as if the spooks had monopolized the furniture business. "Well," the people said, "we have something new!" Something new? This is important, if true. Modern spiritualists persistently urge that the spiritual manifestations of our time are the harbingers of a *new dispensation*. Thousands of years ago Solomon asked: "Is there any thing whereof it may be said, See this is new? It hath been already of old time, which was before us." So of modern spiritualism. From time immemorial the human mind lacked conservativeness, and always tried to push its way into the mysterious continent which God has veiled from mortal sight and fortified against irreverent curiosity. A cursory glance at the records of the past reveals the unimpeachable evidence that from the remotest ages the boundaries of that "undiscovered country, from whose bourne no traveler e'er returns," have been trodden by restless inquisitiveness, anxious to catch the sound of supernatural footfalls, and to learn from the spirit tongues here the wonders that make up the never-changing

hereafter. Spiritualism has coexisted and
harmonized with the densest ignorance, the
most horrible superstitions, the vilest immo-
ralities, and the most atrocious savagery the
world has ever seen. Spiritualistic phenomena, as exhibited in the heathen world, is in
all essential respects similar to the manifestations now observed among spiritualists. In
Greece, temples called Plutonia were consecrated to the spirits of the dead, and rites
conducive to the interchange of spiritualistic
influences were most scrupulously observed.
The profits of those engaged in the business
were enormous. The ancient Greeks employed small tables for purposes of divination,
and planchettes with their attendant phenomena were not uncommon. *Necromancy*, or con-
sultation with the dead, was one of the hea-
thenish customs of ancient Greece. Herod-
otus twenty-five hundred years ago related
the vile communications which Periander, the
tyrant of Corinth and wife-murderer, received
when he consulted the unclean spirits and
insulted every woman in Corinth. Maximus
Tyrius throws a little light on Grecian necromancy when he writes: "There was a place
near Lake Avernus called the Prophetic
Cavern. Persons were in attendance there
who called up ghosts. Any one desiring it

came hither, and having killed a victim and
poured out libations, summoned whatever
ghost he wanted. The ghost came, very faint
and doubtful to the sight, but vocal and prophetic, and having answered the questions
went off." The reported transfigurations of
Imblichus were just as credible as modern
materializations. Thoughtful men in those
times did not hesitate to ascribe them to trickery and fraud, or to natural means, the secret
of which was confined to a few initiated individuals. Cicero, writing of the frivolous
and deceptive character of the Grecian oracles
of those days, denounces them as "*inconsiderate babble, never of any authority with a man of
even moderate capacity.*" The Cumæan Sibyl
tells the Trojan Æneas as much about his
family as any New York medium could, and
from the shade of his father Anchises he re-
ceives responses as remarkable as any that
have ever purported to come from the dead in
our day; and yet Virgil, who describes it all,
calls the maiden possessed of prophetic fancy
"*deranged in intellect.*" Among the Romans
of antiquity the dead men were their heroes
and demi-gods. Consulting the spirits was the
favorite method of finding out who was to
be the next emperor, and doses of poison became so often necessary to fulfill the medium's

prophecy that for public safety the government prohibited these infernal arts, and offenders were severely punished. The Roman law burned alive the mediums, or flung them from the Tarpean Rock. In Sardinia in 184 B.C. the government prosecuted sorcery and condemned two thousand mediums, in order to prevent crime and save the state from the calamities that came through the *lies and poisonings* of the demon-guided wretches. Pliny the naturalist, who wrote about 77 A.D., while he admits some shade of truth in the mystic art, attributes its phenomena to physical causes, and says: " We may be fully assured and boldly conclude that it is a detestable and abominable art, grounded on no certain rules, *full of lies and vanities.*" At last even the common people abandoned the mediums, satisfied that while they could not explain some strange things, there was more of imposture connected with them than could be reconciled with their superhuman claims.

India from the early days has been under the control of mediums. Spiritualism has had time to test its beneficence and progressiveness in India. There spiritualism has been full-blown for ages, and has flourished undisturbed. Now what has the undisputed sway of universal spiritualism accomplished in

India? Not one in 1500 of her 120,000,000 women can read. According to the census of 1881, there were nearly 15,000 women connected with idol temples as prostitutes; 21,000,000 wailing widows, who were given in the hands of brutal men at eight or ten years, are cursed for the death of their husbands; 41,000,000 women are shut up in their zenanas. While the Indians provide food for their sacred cows and monkeys, for serpents and crocodiles, their lepers and helpless and homeless and friendless die uncared for. In 1886 more than 22,000 persons died of snake bites, which they dared not seek to cure lest they might interfere with the ghosts of their grandfathers, who had come back in that shape. Read the story of India's shocking cruelties and despotic castes, its disregard of childhood and degradation of womanhood, and its indifference to human woe and human life, and then ask yourself if we want that kind of "progress" in America. "By their fruits ye shall know them." In China spirit mediums are found everywhere; every house has its ancestral tablets which are worshiped; and what is the result? The mediums have so obstructed progress that they have almost made it a country dead to the civilized world. Their great arguments against railroads and telegraphs are that their grandfathers' graves or their great-grandmothers' ghosts would be disturbed.

Every schoolboy is familiar with the *pow-wowing* stories of our own Indians, and spiritual mediums are common among them. There is not a savage tribe of which we ever had or now have any record which did not claim to have unseen powers with the spirits of the dead.

Spiritualism in America is just as demoralizing as it has been and now is in heathen lands, and everywhere and always instills into the judgment a fanaticism that is revolting to the natural mind. So licentious have been its deeds, and such disgusting and degrading orgies have been enacted under its patronage, that the civil law has often been invoked against it. It has broken up families innumerable, it has pushed young women into profligacy, ruined the financial prosperity of thousands, blinded many eyes to the distinction between right and wrong, and in the lunatic asylums of the United States there are to-day more than ten thousand bleeding victims of this delusion.

VII.

FASHION.

God is a lover of dress. He has put robes of beauty and glory upon all his works. Who can doubt that he will smile upon the evidence of correct taste manifested by his children? No man can afford to disregard appearances. The shabby man loses every year a thousand times the cost of a good suit of clothes. Employers like their people to dress well. It is easier to borrow a hundred dollars in a good suit of clothes than ten cents in an old coat and shabby hat. "The apparel oft proclaims the man." Dress is the visible sign by which the stranger forms his opinion of us. Dress affects a man's manners and morals. A general negligence of dress very often proclaims a corresponding negligence of address. We can scarcely lose self-respect so long as we have respect to appearance; still, the best clothes are often worn by many small-salaried dapper dandies, broken-down merchants, and men

who avoid their tailor because of mortgages
on their clothes. Polonius's advice is good:

"Costly thy habit as thy purse can buy,
But not expressed in fancy; rich, not gaudy."

No true woman will be indifferent to her
appearance; elegance fits woman. The love
of beauty in dress belongs to her; she ought
to take pride in herself and be solicitous to
have all her belongings well chosen and in
good taste. A sloven is abominable. Rudeness is sin. Female loveliness appears to the
best advantage when set off by simplicity of
dress. A woman is best dressed who conducts
herself so that those who have been in her
company shall not recollect what she had on.

I have no sympathy with the "dress-reform-
ers," who glory in their outlandish apparel,
and who are more proud of being "out of the
fashion" than others of being in.

To love dress is not to be a slave of fashion;
to give dress your first thought, your best
time, or all your money, is the evidence of
such slavery. The Bible says, "The body is
more than raiment"; but many people read
the Bible Hebrew-wise—backward—and thus
the general conviction is that raiment is more
than the body.

Fashion tyrannically rules the world. She

pinches the feet with tight shoes, and squeezes the breath out of the body with tight lacing. To be " in the fashion " has made the most famous frauds of the day, and keeps hundreds of men struggling for their commercial existence.

Fashion dwarfs the intellect. Virtue gives up the ghost at her smile. Fashion is the greatest of all liars; she has made society insincere; she has turned society into a great show-room; she has made the poor poorer, and the rich more avaricious. Fashion is New York's leading undertaker, and drives hundreds of hearses to Greenwood.

Dress is a lower beauty, for which the higher beauty should not be sacrificed. The holiest duty is to wear the richest dress on the soul. Woman, with her strong and quick powers, her bold and daring genius, was made for a higher purpose, a nobler use, a grander destiny, than to waste herself on the finified fooleries of fashion. Care more for what you are than what you appear. Let an empty brain, hollow heart, and useless life throw you into a hysterical fit quicker than an old-fashioned bonnet or an ill-fitting dress. Let not fashion close your ears to the appeal of Christ's church, and your eyes to the outstretched hand of the poor. Let not fashion demand of you a style of dress insufficient to keep out the cold and rain, and that will imperil your health. "What! know ye not that your body is the temple of the Holy Ghost which is in you, which ye have of God, and ye are not your own?" Submit to no style which will compromise your modesty. Wear no costume which suggests impure thoughts to the beholder.

It is the instinctive propensity in human nature to decorate. It is right to adorn yourself for your own eyes, for the eyes of your husband, if you are a true wife; if you are a maiden, for the eyes of suitors and companions; but first of all strive to adorn yourself for God's eyes. "Whose adorning let it be the hidden man of the heart, in that which is not corruptible, even the ornament of a meek and quiet spirit, which is in the sight of God of great price." It is worthy of remark that Plato, the loftiest of all Grecian sages, has a passage which strikingly resembles that of the Apostle: "Behavior, and not gold, is the ornament of a woman. To courtesans these things —ornaments and jewels—are advantageous to their catching more admirers; but for a woman who wishes to enjoy the favor of one man good behavior is her proper ornament and not dresses; and you should have the blush upon your countenance, which is the sign of modesty, instead of paint, and worth and sobriety

instead of gold and emeralds." Paul to Titus
says: "That they may adorn the doctrine of
God our Saviour in all things." Even the
great truth of Jesus Christ is here represented
as being susceptible of decoration on the part
of those who profess it. Adorn the Gospel by
useful lives. Say not that the doors of useful
service are closed against you. On every hand
there are hungry to feed and naked to clothe,
and many sick in the hospitals longing for
the sound of woman's voice and the touch of
woman's hand. Seventy-five thousand destitute children to be gathered from our streets
into the Sunday-schools, and three hundred
and forty-five thousand adult heathen in our
own city to be led to the Saviour. How much
better to fill such a sphere to which God calls
you than to flutter like silly butterflies round
milliners, dressmakers, and manicures. Live
for Christ; and with the light and glory of a
true womanhood, fill every day with useful-
ness, as a June day fills the air with the redo-
lence of the roses. The busy Master might
have enthroned himself in a majestic repose,
but his unwearied going about doing good
was a withering rebuke to uselessness. He
honored the useful in the fowls of the air and
in the lilies of the field, but the barren tree
he smote with a curse. He closed the bright

gates of his kingdom in the face of the virgins who preferred indolence and sleep to duty, and the man who wrapped up his gifts in a napkin he sent away to darkness. Oh, you were made for a better companionship than those of whom it is said:

> "Their only labor is to kill time,
>   And labor dire it is, and weary woe;
> They sit, they loll, turn o'er some idle rhyme,
>   Or saunter forth with tottering steps and slow."

Life is not a toy to be played with, a doll to be dressed, an ornament to exhibit, nor a bubble to float in the air, nor an insect to dance on the wave until some wind overtake it; it is not to be a low or dreamy indulgence, not a plague that wastes. Life is a great gift of God, a single opportunity with possibilities vast enough to fill time and eternity with the beatitudes of God, the joy of the angels, and praise of men. Goethe said, "To be useful, that is life." To be useful! How noble, how vast, how sublime, how Christ-like! Henceforth let your life be such as the poet sings:

> "I live for those that love me,
>   For those that know me true,
> For the heaven that smiles above me,
>   And waits my coming too;
> For the cause that lacks assistance,
> For the wrongs that need resistance,
> For the future in the distance,
>   For the good that I can do."

VIII.

THANKSGIVING FOOTBALL.

THE present athletic craze is a reaction from the unwise indifference of the past. In the college halls, where Minerva once held sway, Hercules is now enshrined. The principal talk among college men is football, and our colleges and students take rank, not according to their intellectual attainments and manly character, but according to the size of the biceps muscle and the record in some sort of sport.

Sin committed in the pursuit of pleasure is as sinful as if done for the sake of profit. Thanksgiving Day among the people generally has more to do with the stomach than with the service of God, and with the students especially it has, within several years, become the day when lads get on their first spree.

The sights enacted in our city Thursday night by the college men, the taking possession of saloons, breaking up theaters, blowing horns in people's faces, kissing unprotected women on the public streets, carrying them on their shoulders, drinking themselves drunk, shouting themselves hoarse, and singing with Bowery-tough bravado were a disgrace to our civilization, and the colleges and universities which tolerate such depravities should be consistent and drop the name of Christian.

A thousand wild Indians or monkeys turned loose could not have acted worse than did the respectable sons of praying mothers from colleges and universities founded by Christian patriots. I know this is unpopular talk, but with popularity an honest preacher has simply nothing to do.

That these excessive college sports unfit the students who take part in them for the active work of life is evident from the fact that the majority of our best scholars and most successful men come from the smaller colleges; and if the rich men believe in developing the brains of the country, let them endow the hundreds of small, struggling colleges throughout the land.

On à day set apart by the President of the United States of America for thanksgiving to God for his goodness of the year, cultured gentlemen fight like madmen, goaded by twenty-five thousand people, as if bereft of their reason, sitting nearly five hours in the chilling blasts and yelling themselves hoarse. It shows a tendency in our national life that not only poisons the young, but may plague our fair republic into the grave of the dead nations of history.

IX.

THE most influential factor in our American life is the newspaper. The mother dies, the school is only for our younger days, and the church reaches only a part of the community. The newspaper reaches everybody. It comes to us not only as a news-teller, but also as an oracle. It not only reflects public sentiment, but also shapes it. With few exceptions I can truthfully say the newspapers of this city are daily preaching sobriety, temperance, and honesty in every department of life. Here and there a sensational sheet becomes a sewer and publishes the putrefying details of vice and shame, and magnifies a good man's honest intentions into a public scandal; but the daily press in this city, with few exceptions, has been brave to denounce wrong-doing in high and low places, swift to recognize merit in public life and defend the oppressed, and in its tone and tendency is far above the majority of the life that reads it.

53

There are recreant editors, unfair reporters, and unclean columns, just as there are renegade preachers, praying defaulters, and sanctimonious robbers of widows and orphans. But why is it that the New York "Daily Sewer" exhausts all its editions when its columns are filthiest? The diseased appetites of the people demand unhealthy intelligence, and newpapers are made to sell.

If you want a pure newspaper, don't buy anything but a pure newspaper. The demand will control the supply. Newspaper men will tell you that the greatest trial of their profession is the people's demand for the sensational instead of the sensible. But, gentlemen journalists, it is your sacred mission to lead the people, not to follow them. If you must have a scandal column, label it "Deadly Poison." Benjamin Harris, a pioneer journalist of America, in issuing the prospectus of his "Publick Occurrences, both Foreign and Domestick," published September, 1690, quaintly announces what he conceives to be the duties of an editor. Among these duties he mentions the following:

"Thirdly, that something may be done toward the curing or at least the charming of the spirit of lying which prevails among us, wherefore nothing shall be entered but what we have reason to believe is true, repairing to the best fountains for our information. And when there appears any material mistake in anything that is collected it shall be corrected in the next."

Would to God that every modern editor were as conscientious as old Benjamin Harris! My high regard for the gentlemen of the press justifies me in speaking plainly. Let there be no more catering to the tastes of morbid curiosity, no more intrusion into the privacy of the domestic circle, no personalities, no publication of mere rumors and shocking details of social evils, and let every newspaper man write that only to which he could suffix his name and which he would have his mother, wife, or children read with pride.

X

WHAT TO TEACH A BOY.

THE tender twig is bent in childhood, the spirit is then shaped, the principles are then implanted, and the whole character formed. What to teach a boy? is an important question. Divine wisdom, "Train up a child in the way he should go, and when he is old he will not depart from it," harmonizes with the proverb, "As the twig is bent the tree inclines."

Accuracy.

The great want of Americans is accuracy. Some men live in a kind of mental telescope, through whose magnifying medium every ant-hill is turned into a mountain. General Pope was renowned among his soldiers for his exaggerated rhetoric. In one of the engagements a private was mortally wounded; a chaplain knelt beside him, and opening his Bible at random read about Samson's slaughter of the Philistines with the jaw-bone of an ass. He had not quite finished when the poor fellow interrupted him by saying, "Hold on, chaplain, don't deceive a dying man. Isn't the name of John Pope signed to that?" If a man is to be accurate he must be taught accuracy in his childhood. Let your boy with the first lispings of speech be taught to speak accurately on all subjects, be they trivial or important, and your boy when he becomes a man will scorn to tell a lie. Teach your boy to be sober, honest, modest, and truthful in his observations; by example show him the strict letter of the fact, and do not deal in the marvelous. If your boy has committed a fault or carelessly broken anything, and takes the full blame upon himself and makes no excuses about it, that boy will make every inch a man. Encourage him to tell the truth. Don't whip him because, like a little man, he tells the truth. Whip him—he may lie the next time to escape the whipping.

Consideration for the Feelings of Others.

Teach him to have consideration for the feelings of others—to say not a word, to give not a look, that would cause unnecessary pain. We can understand how that a boy who had never been taught better might carry torpedoes in his pocket and delight in throwing them at the feet of passers-by, but we cannot understand how a man who was well instructed as a boy could do such a thing. And yet there are men who carry torpedoes all their lives, and take exceeding great pleasure in tossing them at people, and enjoy a fiendish delight in seeing them jump.

Contentment.

Children are always happy, joyous, and contented. They sing with the poet,

> "A fig for care, and a fig for woe."

They can, as Shakespeare says,

> "Make a July's day as short as December's."

Indeed, Wordsworth sings of the

> "Sweet childish days that were as long
> As twenty days are now."

Discontent is the bitter in the cup of life. When Pope tells us

> "Man never is, but always to be blessed,"

it would seem as if discontent is the lot of man. Cultivate contentment in your boy. Read to him Charles Swain's poem:

> "If we cannot have all we wish upon earth,
> Let us try to be happy with less if we can.
> If wealth be not always the guerdon of worth,
> Worth, sooner than wealth, makes the happier man.

> "Is it wise to be anxious for pleasures afar,
> And the pleasures around us to slight or decry?
> Asking night for the sun, asking day for the star?
> Let us conquer such faults, or at least let us try.

"There ne'er was delusion more constantly shown,
  Than that wealth every charm of existence can buy;
As long as love, friendship, and truth are life's own,
  All hearts may be happy, if all hearts will try."

Courtesy.

St. Peter enjoins us to "love as brethren, be pitiful, be courteous." A Chinaman was rudely pushed into the mud by an American. He picked himself up very calmly, shook off some of the mud, bowed very politely, and said in a mild, reproving tone of voice, "You Christian, me heathen, alle samee, good-by." Courtesy as a Christian duty has been sorely neglected by Americans. "If a civil word or two will make a man happy," said a French king, "he must be wretched indeed who will not give them to him." William Wirt's letter to his daughter contains the following passage, worthy the attention of boys: "I want to tell you a secret. The way to make yourself pleasing to others is to show them attention. The whole world is like the miller at Mansfield, who cared for nobody—no, not he—because nobody cared for him. And the world would serve you so if you gave them the same cause. Let every one, therefore, see that you do care for them by showing them what Sterne so happily called the small courtesies, in which there is no parade, whose voice is too small to

tease, and which manifest themselves by tender and affectionate looks and little acts of
attention, giving others the preference in every
little enjoyment, at the table, in the field, walking, sitting, and standing."

Decision of Character.

Early instill into your boy's mind decision
of character. Undecided, purposeless boys
make namby-pamby men, useless to themselves and everybody else. They are tossed
to and fro, carried about by every wind of
doctrine. As Dryden puts it,

"Everything by starts, and nothing long."

Teach your boy to have an object in view,
the backbone to go after it, and then stick.
How many men slumber in nameless graves,
or wander through a life more than wasted,
because they had not a worthy purpose, a
patient energy for its accomplishment, a reso-
lution that never flinches, never flies the track.

Revenge.

Teach your boy to disdain revenge. Revenge is a sin "that grows with his growth
and strengthens with his strength."

Your boy goes to school, and he is imposed
upon by another boy. You say to your boy,
"Thrash him if you can." Of course there

is an equal chance that your boy may get thrashed himself. But granting him the victory in the fight, what is gained? Has the bad boy learned a lesson he won't forget, or will it not make him uglier and more malicious than ever? What has your boy gained by the triumph? Anything elevating, ennobling? He has a right to defend himself or get out of the way, but to defend himself by thrashing the other boy is quite another thing. Your boy has gained a little reputation among the other boys as a fighter, which will make him safe from the attacks of smaller boys, but will be very apt to invite the attacks of the larger ones. Your boy's non-resistance, though he received a bloody nose or a broken head, would have made him a self-controller, a morally courageous, noble man, and taught the bad boy a lesson in morals and religion he would never forget. Strike the balance, fathers and boys, and see on which side of the balance sheet you would rather be—on the side of moral courage or of brute force.

Honor.

There is nothing that improves a boy's character so much as putting him on his honor—trusting to his honor. I have little hope for the boy who is dead to the feeling of honor.

The boy who needs to be continually looked after is on the road to ruin. If treating your boy as a gentleman does not make him a gentleman, nothing else will.

Independence.

Let your boy wait upon himself as much as possible. The more he has to depend upon himself, the more manly a little fellow he will show himself. Self-dependence will call out his energies, bring into exercise his talents. Pythagoras says, "Ability and necessity dwell near each other." It is not in the hot-house, but on the rugged Alpine cliffs, where the storms beat most violently, that the toughest plants grow. So is it with man. The wisest charity is to help a boy to help himself. Let him never hear any language but this: "You have your own way to make, and it depends on your own exertion whether you starve or live."

A Trade.

It is a rule in the imperial family of Germany that every young man shall learn a trade, going through a regular apprenticeship till he is able to do good journey-work. This is required because in the event of unforeseen changes it is deemed necessary to a manly independence that the heir-apparent or a prince of the blood should be conscious of ability of making his own way in the world. This is an honorable custom, worthy of universal American emulation. The Jews wisely held the maxim that every youth, whatever his position in life, should learn some trade. Franklin says, "He that hath a trade hath an estate." Work, however looked down upon by people who cannot perform it, is an honorable thing; it may not be very profitable, but honorable it always is, and there is nothing to be ashamed of about it. The man who has reason to be ashamed is the one who does nothing, or is always on the lookout for an easy berth with good pay and no work. Let the dandy, whose conceit greatly exceeds his brains, be ashamed of his cane and kid gloves, but never let a man who works be ashamed of his hard hands. Christ was a carpenter, and Paul was a tent-maker. "Mere gentility sent to market won't buy a peck of oats."

Half-asleep Boys.

Encourage your boy to be industrious. Don't allow him to grow up half-asleep-dead-alive. Boys, don't live in hope with your arms folded. Roll up your sleeves and put your shoulders to the wheel and fortune will smile on you. Have something to do, then do it as if the whole world waited on your doing it.

Perseverance.

Lucky for the boy who can say, "In the bright lexicon of youth there is no such word as *fail.*" Out upon weather-cock men, who change with every wind! Give us men like mountains, who change the winds. You cannot at one dash fly into eminence. You must hammer it out by steady and rugged blows. A man can get what he wants if he pays the price—persistent, plodding perseverance. Never doubt the result; victory will be yours. There may be ways to fortune shorter than the old, dusty highway, but the staunch men in the community all go on this road. If you want to do anything, don't stand back shivering and thinking of the cold; jump in and scramble through. Push and pull!

Fathers' Companionship with Boys.

Happy is the father who is happy in his boy, and happy is the boy who is happy in his father. Some fathers are not wise. They reserve all their social charms for strangers, are dull at home, forbid their children to go into the nicely furnished rooms, make home as irksome as possible, forget that they were once young, deny their children every amusement and pleasure. Many of the sons of most pious fathers turn out badly because they are surfeited with severe religion, not the religion of Christ, who was himself reproved by the prototypes of such severe men.

We do not remember ever having read of a father's home-life more beautiful and instructive than that of Charles Kingsley: "Because the rectory-house was on low ground, the rector of Eversley, who considered violation of the divine laws of health a sort of acted blasphemy, built his children an outdoor nursery on the 'Mount,' where they kept books, toys, and tea-things, spending long, happy days on the highest and loveliest point of moorland in the glebe; and there he would join them when his parish work was done, bringing them some fresh treasure picked up in his walk—a choice wild-flower or fern or rare beetle, sometimes a lizard or a field-mouse, ever waking up their sense of wonder, calling out their powers of observation, and teaching them lessons out of God's great green book without their knowing they were learning. Out-of-doors and indoors the Sundays were the happiest days to the children, though to their father the hardest.

"When his day's work was done there was

always the Sunday walk, in which each bird
and plant and brook was pointed out to the
children as preaching sermons to Eyes, such
as were not even dreamt of by people of the
No-eye species. Indoors the Sunday picture-
books were brought out and each child chose
its subject for the father to draw, either some
Bible story, or bird or beast or flower."

Kingsley had a horror of corporal punishment, not merely because it tends to produce
antagonism between parent and child, but because he considered more than half the lying
of children to be the result of fear of punishment. "Do not train a child," he said, "as
men train a horse, by letting anger and punishment be the first announcement of his having sinned. If you do, you induce two bad
habits: first, the boy regards his parent with
a kind of blind dread, as a being who may be
offended by actions which to him are innocent,
and whose wrath he expects to fall upon him
at any moment in his most pure and unselfish
happiness; next, and worse still, the boy learns,
not to fear sin, but the punishment of it, and
thus he learns to lie."

He had no "moods" with his family, for he
cultivated, by strict discipline in the midst of
worries and pressing business, a disengaged
temper that always enabled him to enter into

other people's interests, and especially into children's playfulness. " I wonder," he would say, " if there is so much laughing in any other home in England as in ours." He became a light-hearted boy in the presence of his children. When broken toys and nursery griefs were taken to his study, he was never too busy to mend the toy or dry the tears.

How blessed is the son who can speak of his father as Charles Kingsley's eldest son does. "'Perfect love casteth out fear,' was the motto," he says, " on which my father based his theory of bringing up children. From this, and from the interest he took in their pursuits, their pleasures, trials, and even the petty details of their every-day life, there sprang up a friendship between father and children that increased in intensity and depth with years. To speak for myself, he was the best friend—the only true friend I ever had. At once he was the most fatherly and the most unfatherly of fathers—fatherly in that he was our most intimate friend and our self-constituted adviser; unfatherly in that our feeling for him lacked that fear and restraint that make boys call their father ' the governor.' Ours was the only household I ever saw in which there was no favoritism. Perhaps the brightest picture of the past that I look back to now is the draw-

ing-room at Eversley in the evenings, when
we were all at home and by ourselves. There
he sat, with one hand in mother's, forgetting
his own hard work in leading our fun and
frolic, with a kindly smile on his lips and a
loving light in the bright gray eye that made
us feel that in the broadest sense of the word
he was our father." Writing to his wife from
the seaside, where he had gone in search of
health, he says: "This place is perfect, but
it seems a dream and imperfect without you.
Kiss the darling ducks of children for me."

However busy you are, find a few moments
at least every day to romp with your boy.
The father who is too dignified to carry his
boy pick-back, or, like Luther, sing and dance
with his children, or, like Chalmers, trundle
the hoop, lacks not only one of the finest elements of greatness, but fails in one of his
plainest duties to his children. One of the in-
alienable rights of your children is happiness
at your hands. Remember that the children
belong as much to you as to your wife, and it
is only just to her that the little time you are
in the house you should relieve her of those
cares that are her daily portion.

You cannot afford to let your boy grow up
without weaving yourself into the memory of
his golden days. Norman McLeod says: "O

sunshine of youth, let it shine on! Let love flow out fresh and full, unchecked by any rule but what love creates, and pour itself down without stint into the young heart. Make the days of boyhood happy, for other days of labor and sorrow must come, when the blessing of those dear eyes and clasping hands and sweet caresses will, next to the love of God from whence they flow, save the man from losing faith in the human heart, help to deliver him from the curse of selfishness, and be an Eden in the evening when he is driven forth into the wilderness of life." Another writes: "The richest heritage that parents can give is a happy childhood, with tender memories of father and mother. This will brighten the coming days when the children have gone out from the sheltering home, it will be a safeguard in times of temptation and a conscious help amid the stern realities of life."

Boys on the Streets.

Don't turn your boys out to spend the night —you don't know where. There are thousands of parents in this city who think that their boys never drink, but there is not a gilded saloon with which the boys are not familiar. There are many young men who, when they return to their fathers' houses, are supposed to have been visiting respectable friends of the family. This is a mere guise. They would not dare to tell the truth as to where and with whom they had been. Don't allow your boy to go at night to see the sights or to find pleasure in the amusements of the city unless you go with him, until he is grown to man's estate and his habits are formed.

There are many things of which ignorance is bliss and wisdom folly—things which a man cannot learn without being damaged all his life. "As an eel, if he were to wriggle across your carpet, would leave a slime which no brush can take off, so there are many things which no person can know and ever recover from the knowledge of."

The Friend of Liberty and Pleasure.

I am known, and want to be known, as the friend of liberty and pleasure. I rebuke those who would turn that young and joyous creature into the stiff and silent statue, the monk-like figure, or the unsmiling devotee. It is a cold, cheerless, heartless asceticism and not Christianity that cannot see the boy's sparkling eye, his sunlit countenance, hear his elastic step, the merry note of his laughter, and the music of his cheerful voice. I believe in fun. There is fun, innocent fun, and you

don't have to go in the paths of sin to find it.
I appreciate hilarity, good jokes, and fun.
Hear it, boys! There is glorious fun in this
world, and on the side of right, in the path of
virtue. Getting up in the morning with a
splitting headache, disordered liver, and shattered nerves, turned out of employment, cast
down in spirits, character wrecked, father disgraced, mother's heart broken. Alas for that
kind of fun! O my soul, stand back from
such fun! If you want to make your boy's
destruction sure, give him unwatched liberty
after dark.

Henry Ward Beecher writes: "I do not believe in bringing up the young to know life,
as it is said. I should just as soon think of
bringing up a child by cutting some of the
cords of his body and lacerating his nerves,
and scarring and tattooing him, and making an
Indian out of him outright as an element of
beauty, as I should think of developing his
manhood by bringing him up to see life—to
see its abominable lusts, to see its hideous in-
carnations of wit, to see its infernal wicked-
ness, to see its extravagant and degrading
scenes, to see its miserable carnalities, to see
its imaginations set on fire of hell, to see all
those temptations and delusions which lead to
perdition. Nobody gets over the sight of these

things. They who see them always carry scars. They are burned. The scar remains. And to let the young go out where evil appears, where the frequenters of dens of iniquity can come within their reach, to let them go where the young gather together to cheer with bad wit, to let them go where they will be exposed to such temptations—why, a parent is insane that will do it. To say, ' A child must be hardened; he has got to get tough somehow, and you may as well put him in the vat and let him tan '—is that family education? Is that Christian nurture? Is that bringing a child up in the nurture and admonition of the Lord?"

XI.

IN company with a trusty friend, one of earth's greatest blessings, I visited Water Street when the thermometer registered ninety degrees in the shade. I started early that I might gain some knowledge of the "free-ice" stations.

What blessings this charity brings to these dark places of abject poverty! To stand for an hour at any one of these stations and watch the creatures who creep there to receive the blessing of fifteen pounds of ice, to behold the eagerness with which they make approach, the anxiety with which they push forward, the glistening gladness in their eyes as they bear off the trophy, is only to comprehend in a small measure the good done by this practical philanthropy.

Here they come and crowd, men, women and children, of all kindreds and tongues, the dwarf, scurvy and scrub of humanity. Sometimes the crowd is so dense that angry com-

73

petition follows. Boys and girls with emaci-
ated bodies, feverish lips, hollow eyes, dirty
all over, are on the outside and watching for
the chips of ice that fall to the ground. One
little girl to secure her prize sat on her ice
until her competitors had withdrawn.

This free-ice station on Water Street is a
chunk of a heaven on the brink of a hell. As
I stood near the unwashed wretchedness, my
high hope and fervent prayer was that the
generosity of New Yorkers might next year
open such stations in every needy part of our
city.

You need not walk far down Water Street
to find outlandish sights. Between a barrel
and a box there was stretched on a stone, with
head on a door-sill, a woman, a mother, it
seemed—

> "A drinking dame,
> A sight of shame!"

Yet how sadly common is this spectacle in
Water Street! I write of this misery because
my memory refuses to forget this picture of
pity—this blasphemy on womankind, eyes
filled with water, asleep, pimpled cheeks and
red nose, telling the sad story of her sin and
shame.

> "Bacchus well his sheep he knows,
> For he marks them on the nose."

But the poor little babe would draw tears
to the eyes of our gayest butterflies of society
and the masculine grasshoppers which dance
attendance upon them. It was ragged, dirty;
want of food was manifested in its sunken
little eyes, its withered cheeks, its bony little
fingers, and its frail little ankles. There was
the restless little fellow moaning and groaning
to get his dinner from a breast whose mater-
nity the demon drink had clutched by the
throat and choked to death. A diamond in a
gutter! If drunkenness follows hard on the
heels of moderation, so a harlot may carry a
rose on her bosom.

A few doors from the drunken mother and
unfortunate babe was seen a little boy about
seven years old, comely, clean and bright, a
little cherub that you would like to have play
with your children. His shoes were delicate,
his stockings matched·his velvet suit, and
his head was covered with a new white hat.
There was an artistic knot in his ribbon neck-
tie. He was sweet! I instinctively said,
"That boy has a Christian mother, or there is
a mystery about his life, a romance of some
kind. The parentage of that boy is not found
in the slums." That boy came in the ruin of
a beautiful young woman. In her face can
still be traced the lines of beauty. Shame has

driven her and her neat little care to this
street, there to wither and melt like snow in
the spring, shedding burning tears of sadness
over man's villainy and woman's inhumanity
to woman, which

"Has made countless thousands mourn."

Among many species of animals, if one of
their number is wounded and falls, he is at
once torn to pieces by his fellows. Traces of
this animal cruelty are seen in men to-day,
but especially in women. Let a woman fall
from virtue and nine-tenths of her sisters will
turn and tear her to pieces, and the next day
the man who robbed her of virtue, broke her
parents' hearts, and drove her to the street,
will be smiled on and almost congratulated
on his success. The cruelty of woman to
woman is perfectly wolfish. Shame! oh,
shame! Reverse the .action. Loathing for
the gay Lothario who accomplished her ruin,
and tenderness for the wounded sister.

As the silver in the raw and rough matrix
still sparkles, so there are glimpses of nobility
in the ruins of the slums. Here in the junc-
tion of the street and alley were two little girls
about six years of age, short and chubby, with
round faces and wild hair. They were dressed

each in a single garment of calico, which clothed them, in spots, to their knees. The dirt seemed to be glued on them. The moment I was looking at them, one had found in the gutter a piece of watermelon rind with a slight margin of red in it. She was so pleased. With generosity sparkling in her eyes, she broke it in two and gave the half to her playmate. While looking at her little friend with an affectionate eye, she caught a glimpse of me. Not used to people to whose kind call the children troop, they ran behind a barrel to enjoy their luxury. Here were the signs of the noblest traits in human nature—impulses of the divinest character. What seeds of possibilities! Give the little ones a chance to become decent, to be suitably clothed, wellfed, educated, and Christianized, and they will be a blessing to their race. But let them be kicked into a grudge against society, snubbed, starved, and sunk in crime, they will grow up to curse mankind and hate all that is good.

There are seventy-five thousand children in New York City worse than homeless, friendless and godless. It is this population that furnishes seventy-five per cent. of our criminals. If we do not Christianize them, they will heathenize us.

We send good missionaries to save the babies of China, but let the devil take the babies at home. A minister lately told a pathetic story of the miseries of infant life in China—of the babes who were left in the streets at night to die of exposure; four thousand were saved by the missionary women. Now that preacher did not know that the same thing is going on at home. Not a willful exposure to the cold and heat, but a compulsory neglect. Could that preacher go with me through some of the benighted streets of New York and Brooklyn, he could see hundreds of babes in the agonies of death, dying by the inch of heat, of cold, of want of food and care. Let him see their puny and skinny little hands, the limbs withering with starvation, eyes sunken or bulging out of their sockets. They are eaten up with fever and with filth. Have we home missionaries to go out and look after these? Do our churches take up contributions to minister to these little ones of our own cities? I go in for missions; but so long as there are, according to reliable data, three hundred and forty-five thousand persons in New York City without the Gospel and the benefits of a Christian civilization, I am opposed to a cent going to Zanzibar or Timbuctoo. Still it must be confessed that as a rule the men who give nothing to foreign missions give nothing to home missions.

The police were noticeably absent from Water Street. Abandoned women are allowed to stand in the doors to solicit and invite the innocent into their dens. Vice flourishes in the Fourth Precinct with the most brazen-faced audacity, either through police complicity or police stupidity.

The houses in Water Street are not fit for habitation. No conveniences, bad ventilation, filthy sewers and unclean alleys; whole families occupy one room, eat, drink, cook and sleep in a room ten feet by ten. I have found instances of from ten to seventeen people huddled together in one or two rooms, the whole space not being more than ten by twenty feet. A dozen odors rush into your nostrils at the same time, and each one distinct from the other. The way they cook in the slums is a study. They do not know what it is to taste a good meal. Weary with toil, they crave for something to eat and drink. They drink because they have not enough to eat, or because what they eat does not satisfy.

It seems to me that what is needed very much is a mission to teach them how to look well to the ways of the household. It is not theology they want so much as some knowledge in the sciences of *bake-ology, boil-ology, cook-ology, stitch-ology,* and *mend-ology.*

To work successfully in the slums a great deal of sanctified common sense is needed. A missionary in Water Street told me that not long ago a minister came to her and told her that, walking down Water Street, he was invited to enter the abode of one of these demons of darkness. He went in and began to talk of home, holiness, and heaven. The girl burst into tears. He thought his words were doing the good intended, and that he might have a better chance to speak and pray with her he hired a room, paying a dollar for it, that he might unmolested show her the way of life. This man was good, but he was green. He had learning, but it was of a kind that makes its possessors so magnificently ridiculous that the simplest plowman could perceive his shortness of wit. He is as much out of place in the pulpit as if a salmon should climb a tree.

In the evening I visited the old McAuley Mission. I heard the testimony of drunkards redeemed, some of long and others of recent experience. Many bore the marks of having not yet had time to get good clothes and to wear off the effects of the distilled damnation which had well-nigh destroyed them. These men did not parade their sins in their testimonies, but praised God.   They impressed me with the fact that their godliness was not only from the lips outward.   It was not the noisy zeal that sought the praise of man.   " A handful of holy life is worth a ton of tall talk."

XII.

" The righteous shall flourish like a palm-tree."—DAVID.

THE palm branches shoot upward, and there are none that grow out of the side as in other trees; so the Christian seeks the things above, where Christ dwells. Rearing its stem and diffusing its shade as a shelter over the exhausted traveler, how beautifully does this tree exemplify the Christian who becomes a shade to the friendless, the destitute, and the afflicted. Like the palm, the Christian must become a shade to others.

The palm-tree yields abundant fruit. "The dates hung from these trees," says a learned traveler, "in such large and tempting clusters that we climbed to the tops of some of them and carried away with us large branches with their fruit. Wherever the date-tree is found in these dreary deserts, it not only presents a supply of salutary food for men and camels, but nature has so wonderfully contrived the

82

plant that its first offering is accessible to man alone, and the mere circumstance of its presence in all seasons of the year is a never-failing indication of fresh water near its roots. A considerable part of the inhabitants of Europe, Arabia, and Persia subsist almost entirely upon its fruit. They boast also of its medicinal virtues. Their camels feed upon the date-stones; from the leaves and branches are made an astonishing variety of domestic furniture and utensils; from the fibers of the boughs are manufactured thread, ropes and rigging; the body of the tree furnishes fuel; and from one variety of the tree meal has been extracted and has been used for food." Are not thus the righteous pictured forth by this tree? Eyes to the blind, ears to the deaf, feet to the lame, clothes to the naked, food to the hungry—they are known, like the secret wells of the desert, by the living verdure about them; like the palm, whose " presence is a never-failing indication of fresh water near its roots," their presence is felt by the happiness they produce, the good seeds they sow, and the atmosphere of light and holiness which diffuse a grateful fragrance through all with whom they come in contact.

The palm-tree grows in the purest soil; it will not grow in filthy places. The righteous flourish best in a pure soil, "in the garden," the house of God, where the pure Gospel is preached.

The palm-tree when young is a very weak plant; it can hardly stand by itself; and therefore usually three or four are planted together, and by that means they strengthen one another. "They that be planted in the house of the Lord shall flourish in the courts of our God." The righteous when first converted are as babes in Christ; weak and feeble, they need the help and support of their brethren; but when planted together in God's vineyard they strengthen one another, thus showing the excellency of Christian fellowship. "Strengthen ye the weak hands and confirm the feeble knees." Palm-trees join and clasp and grow one to the other, and by that means flourish exceedingly. So the righteous, being planted together in the same church in gospel fellowship, ought so to join, clasp and cleave in love to one another so to become as it were one tree, and thus be made strong.

The palm-tree is always green. It does not cast its leaves or fade. "And he shall be like a tree planted by the rivers of water, that bringeth forth his fruit in his season; his leaf also shall not wither; and whatsoever he doeth shall prosper." The Lord's trees are all evergreens, yet, unlike evergreens in our country, they are all fruit-bearers.

The palm-tree is uninfluenced by those alternations of the seasons which affect other trees. Winter's copious rains do not rejoice it overmuch, nor does it droop under the drought and burning sun of summer. There it stands, with its tall and verdant canopy and the silvery flashes of its waving plumes, looking calmly down upon the world below, and patiently yielding its large clusters of golden fruit from generation to generation. It brings forth fruit in old age—the best dates are produced when the tree is from fifty to one hundred years old.

> "The plants of grace shall ever live;
> Nature decays, but grace must thrive;
> Time, that doth all things else impair,
> Still makes them flourish strong and fair."

The young Christian is lovely, like a tree in the blossoms of spring; the aged Christian is valuable, like a tree in autumn bending with ripe fruit. In the old disciple we may therefore look for something superior—more deadness to the world, more disposition to make sacrifice for the sake of others, more richness of experience, and more confidence in God.

Neither weight nor violence can make the palm grow crooked, but the more it is op-

posed, the more it flourishes. So, if we bear
up bravely under trial, we give evidence to the
world that our piety is invincible and calm.
Like the waves in the storm, the righteous
are frequently tossed to and fro by the trials
of life; but, like them, they are uninjured,
for soon the tempest of suffering subsides, and
the light of heaven sleeps upon their bosom.

XIII.

To show the young men of my congregation
what moral contagion is hidden behind the
glazed windows and curtained doors of the
grog-shops of New York City, I secured, at
various times, samples from some sample-
rooms, such as would be sold to any casual
customer, and a careful analysis developed
the following results:

A half-pint of gin contained neutral spirits, rotten corn, juniper-berries, turpentine
and vitriol. I put a match to a small quantity
of this Holland (?) gin, and the blue flame it
burned would have done a drinker good. I
took the white of an egg, quite equal in substance to the fluids of the brain; I poured
over it a little of this gin, and the albumi-
nous substance slowly congealed, thickened
and clotted. It lost its clearness and became
stringy and compact, and finally hardened.
It is the chemical effect of alcohol on vital
substance, exactly what goes on in your brain

to a greater or less degree when you drink
alcohol in any shape or form. A raw oyster,
which is very digestible, whiskey hardened
and toughened as leather. Such in a degree
is the effect produced by the contact of alcohol with the stomach.

In half a pint of whiskey we found neutral
spirits, glycerine, sulphate of zinc, chromic
acid, unslacked lime, creosote and fusel oil.
As to fusel oil, it is poisonous enough, so
that, according to Dr. Blythe, the highest
authority on adulterations, "fifteen drachms
evaporated in a box where a cat had been confined rendered the animal insensible in less
than an hour. Forty drops of fusel oil ad-
ministered to a kitten after seventeen minutes caused palpitation of the heart, irregular
breathing, and in twenty-two minutes uncon-
sciousness. A rabbit was killed by two
drachms taken in the stomach. Reasoning
from these experiences, anything like half a
grain of fusel oil, per ounce of whiskey, is certainly extremely injurious to health."

The brandy sold in the average saloon is
made up of the refuse of grapes, fusel oil,
methyl alcohol, tannin, sulphuric acid, lead,
copper, zinc and cayenne pepper.

Port-wine contained neutral spirits, glycerine, licorice, flavored with zinc, mercury,

antimony and several acids, fortified by brandy plastered with gypsum, and mixed with inferior wines; salt of tartar and ether are often added to give an appearance of age, and alum to increase the brilliancy of hue. There is perhaps nearly a hundred times as much " port-wine " (so-called from Oporto) sold and drunk as can be made from all the grapes raised in the region of Oporto, including the whole Douro Valley.

If the whole Douro Valley were a thousand miles long, instead of only sixty, it could not furnish grapes enough to provide all this ocean of port-wine. The whole world is drinking wine out of the handful of grapes grown on the banks of a small creek in Portugal!

Madeira *grows* 30,000 barrels of wine yearly, and America *drinks* 50,000 barrels of Madeira wine! A Madeira wine is made in this country at a profit of five hundred per cent. which few can tell from the genuine, by mixing with cider, rain-water, sulphuric acid and other in- gredients. California wine is made in New Jersey, sold at twenty cents per gallon, and at a thousand per cent. profit.

The vineyards of Europe have been devas- tated by the phylloxera and various diseases. In France and Italy three-fourths of the vine- yards have been wholly destroyed within five years, and the remaining fourth is rapidly yielding to the plague. Five years ago Spain and Germany produced six times the amount of grapes harvested last year. The vinelands of Europe, where wine has been produced continuously for one thousand years, are for the most part worn out. The Old World will soon have to rely on us for the production of its supply of wines. Our country is already the largest wine-growing district in the world. We furnish a million times more baskets of champagne (with exact imitations of foreign brands) than are put up out of the pure juice in all the champagne districts of Europe. In California alone there are forty-five thousand acres planted in vines, and last year there were produced from this acreage eighty-seven million gallons of wine, valued at twenty-four million dollars.

Beer is frightfully adulterated. Read the "Reports on the Examination of Beers," by the State Board of Health. Barley, malt, hops, yeast, and water, only, make pure beer. J. P. Battershall, Chemist of the United States Laboratory, says that "any ingredient other than these must be regarded as an adulterant."

The brewer's own book, "Preparation of Malt and Fabrication of Beer," by Thausing,

Schwarz & Bauer, says: "The reason for using malt surrogates will always be to reduce the expense of brewing beer." When the fight was made in the House of Representatives against "the use of substitutes for barley, malt and hops in the manufacture of beer," fierce opposition to the bill came from the Glen Cove Starch Company. The business of this company was the manufacture of glucose. Glucose is a chemical result of starch and sulphuric acid. Its economic uses are none other save as a substitute for better materials—an adulterant and a debaser.

Read the brewer's book already mentioned, also "Brewing," in the Library of Universal Knowledge, Child's "Every Man His Own Brewer," and Morice's "Brewing Malt Liquors," and you will find substitutes something like these:

Ingredients of a warming nature.—Pepper, capsicum, cloves, ginger, spice, vinegar; acetic, tartaric, citric, butyric, nitric, sulphuric and prussic acids; nitric and acetic ethers; spirits of niter; oils of vitriol, turpentine, cassia, caraway, cloves; extracts of japonica, of bitter almonds, orris root and angelican root, grains of paradise, poppy seeds, aloes, cochineal, black ants and Spanish juice.

To give taste and astringency.—Bruised

raisins, dried blackberries, peaches and cherries, orange peel, coriander seed, white oak bark, tannic acid, kino, rhatany, catechu, caraway, cardamom and fennel seeds, wormwood, alum, copperas, sulphate of iron and sulphate of copper.

To prevent sourness.—Use sugar, honey, molasses, licorice, alum, opium, gentian, quassia, aloes, cocculus indicus (the rankest poison without any known antidote), eggshells, sulphate of lime, nutgalls, etc.

To correct unnatural tastes.—Lime-water, carbonate of lime and of soda, nitrate of potash, caustic potash, saleratus, sugar of lead, etc.

For coloring matters.—Burnt sugar, beet juice, dried apples and peaches, elder-berries, molasses, red saunders, logwood and sulphuric acid. This catalogue suffices to account for the fact that many breweries (laboratories) contain a well-equipped drug-store as part of their outfit. Think of introducing into the stomach such fluid nastiness and poisons!

Some of my readers may recall the wrathful challenge that the chairman of the United States Brewers' Association thundered at the writer through a letter in the New York *Herald*, for the proof that the American beer was as dangerously adulterated as charged.

He admitted that foreign substances were put in beer "to keep it," and only denied they were dangerous. The American brewers claim that pure lager made out of nothing but barley, malt, hops, yeast, and water will not "keep." It "keeps" in Bavaria and other countries which export beer to America. Laws there prevent other ingredients than those named being used. Why will it not "keep" here? In one of our daily papers there appeared recently an advertisement of the leading brewery in America, which had the following: "Corn Beer Manufacturers 'not in it.' No corn or corn preparations are used in brewing. Our motto is: 'Not How Cheap, but How Good.'" Why have the brewers always opposed a statutory definition that beer should be made from barley, malt, hops, yeast, and water, as prescribed by the laws of other countries?

XIV

WHY WE SHOULD SERVE CHRIST.

THE life of a Christian is a life of love from the beginning to the end. St. John tells us "we love him because he first loved us." The Greek words "we love" are not in the indicative but in the subjunctive, making this an exhortation, "Let us love him because he first loved us." Our hearts must be conscious of a personal love toward Christ before we can love him. It is possible to serve Christ as a duty rather than as a privilege. We do many things under the idea that God expects it of us, and we are afraid to resist his will. So long as we love Christ merely because he loves us, our motives are actually selfish. God appeals to this self-love in our heart, but only that through it he might lead us up to better things. When we begin to recognize the claims of God we may, like Moses, have "respect unto the recompense of the reward"; but a passionate love for Jesus must follow after we have stretched our hands to embrace him

94

as the Saviour we require. The true ground of love to Christ is the excellence of his own character, apart from the question whether we are to be benefited or not. The highest ground of exhortation to love Christ is not the benefits which we are to receive, but because his character is infinitely worthy of love. So thought Francis Xavier:

> "I love thee, O my God! but not
>   For what I hope thereby;
> Nor yet because who love thee not
>   Must die eternally.
> I love thee, O my God! and still
>   I ever will love thee,
> Solely because my God thou art,
>   Who first hast lovèd me.

> "For me to lowest depths of woe
>   Thou didst thyself abase;
> For me didst bear the cross, the shame,
>   And manifold disgrace;
> For me didst suffer pains unknown,
>   Blood sweat and agony,
> Yes, death itself,—all, all for me,
>   For me, thine enemy.

> "Then shall I not, O Saviour mine!
>   Shall I not love thee well?
> Not with the hope of winning heaven,
>   Nor of escaping hell;
> Not with the hope of earning aught,
>   Not seeking a reward,
> But freely, freely as thyself
>   Hast lovèd me, O Lord!"

XV.

HERESY trials have been few and far between in our theological history. Lyman Beecher's trial stands first, and that record should be kept sacred in our history, along with the history of the burning of witches in Salem and the hanging of Quakers on Boston Common, to show to what bigoted extremes the self-styled defenders of orthodoxy can go. Albert Barnes was compelled to give up his pulpit for a time because some passage was found in his splendid commentaries which was construed into teaching a disbelief in a limited atonement. The church remembers that trial with the blush of shame. David Swing was ruthlessly driven from the pale of the church because he said things that did not square with the exact phrases of the Westminster Confession. That trial was a spiritual calamity to Chicago. The majority to bring Dr. Briggs to trial was not brought about by the clergymen, but by the vote of laymen distinguished mainly for inquisitorial dictation. Parliamentary decorum was disregarded in a fashion that would disgrace a political caucus. I do not indorse all the views of Dr. Briggs. My pulpit is an orthodox carriage, from which I do not believe in firing a heterodox gun. But the trouble is that every man considers his *doxy* orthodoxy. I believe that free research and free speech is the sacred right of the pulpit, and individuality of thought in religion the immortal principle of Protestantism. The Westminster divines were as much divided as the New York Presbytery on the Articles in the Confession of Faith, and the things that they carried were carried by a mere majority, with strong protest against them. Shall what they did more than two hundred years ago constitute the spectacles through which we are to look upon our Bibles to-day? The man for the hour is not he who lives to defend the Thirty-nine Articles or the Five Institutes, but he who lives to make this world wiser, holier and happier. The creeds of the middle ages have no more to do with the Christianity of Christ than the battle of Marathon had with the defeat of Benjamin Harrison. The minister who gets into a raging fever of passion because one of his brethren dared to express an opinion not indorsed by the church fathers (church grandmothers!) is certainly a queer being to live in this progressive age. Just so long as the church busies herself punishing men for having an opinion there will be indifference to religion, and the world will shrug its shoulders at the clergy and say with Dean Swift: "There are three sexes—men, women and preachers." Animosities among the followers of the Prince of Peace! What an inconsistency! How unfortunate it is for Christianity for her ministers to spend year after year in wrangling, when in New York City alone there are three hundred and forty-five thousand souls as unreached by the Gospel as are the blackest blacks in blackest Africa. The forces of iniquity are presenting a solid, compact front, while Christian men debate, wrangle and quarrel about non-essentials. Now this thing must stop. Public sentiment is against it, and the man who starts unnecessary discussion upon theological points acts wrongly. Its direct tendency is to prevent the conversion of souls. It serves to distract the thoughts of those who might otherwise become serious, and leads them into fruitless discussion. It tends to separate men who would otherwise love each other. Oh, for a divine voice to utter the command, "Peace, be still!"

XVI.

SPIRITUALISM is a mixture of puerility and stolidity, a superfluous, superficial and superstitious speculation. It converts the dead into busybodies, changes the beatified into phantom tramps and spectral gossips. Spiritualists make it their proud boast that they are free from the bondage of superstition, and singularly enough greedily render their judgment captive to the gossip, garrulity and guesses of contemptible outcasts.

The main staple of spiritualism is deception. No wonder it chooses the darkness. What a silly thing it is! Picture to yourself a circle of men and women—lights out—sitting with clasped hands, singing dolorously, "John Brown's body lies mouldering in the grave, while his soul goes marching on." And for what? To bring down the glory-enthroned father, mother, husband, wife or child; crawling under the table, ringing tea-bells before supper is ready.

It is a sad sight. I do not wonder that an old Greek philosopher said, "The diviners" (that is, spiritualists) "make one think that man, instead of being the most intelligent, is the most stupid of animals."

Mediums, clairvoyants and "psychometric readers" denounce one another as frauds, and in this one particular they tell the truth. Who are your professional mediums? Would those who visit them receive them into their homes on terms of social equality? Suppose our departed dead could communicate with us, would they go to entire strangers, to people with whom when living they would not associate, and tell to such social outcasts and arrant, unmitigated humbugs the most sacred things—things which if they were living they would tell in no ears but ours?

The very thought of such a possibility is degrading and insulting to the memory of the sainted dead. Would it be consistent with the character of a holy God to give his revelation for a financial consideration through such universally acknowledged disreputable characters by sending his spirit under a table or into a cabinet to peep and mutter at men?

The messages that purport to come from the spirit world make us think our departed friends had an attack of softening of the brain after they became spirits.

The cunningly devised and cleverly executed tricks employed in spiritualism have all been exposed and proven frauds.

Spiritualists claim that their doctrine is important to society; that it proves the future life. But if that future life is to be judged by the disclosures made of it by the representatives of spiritualism, we are forced to conclude that the inhabitants of that future life are souls in the process of losing their mental powers—souls destined soon to become extinct; and under such circumstances eternity is not attractive enough to convince a man that it is worth striving for.

The Bible teaches that men may deal with spirits and be entirely under their control, but it also tells us the character of the spirits, "lying wonders," "seducing spirits and doctrines of devils which will shipwreck our faith," "wicked," "unclean," "familiar spirits," "possessed with devils," and this is how God speaks of this delusion: "I will be a swift witness against the sorcerer." "There shall be among you a consulter of familiar spirits, or wizard, or necromancer, for they that do these things are an abomination unto the Lord."

The Bible speaks of angels appearing to men. But angels are not the spirits of dead men, they are an entirely different order of beings. When angels appeared to men no mediums were used, no admission charged, no circles formed, no turning-down of lights, no cabinets, no planchettes. The angels came directly to the persons to whom they were sent, and never in a darkened room.

The Bible tells us all we need to know about the hereafter. It is sacrilege to pry into that which is none of our business.

XVII.

THE first step the devil takes in seeking to compass a young man's destruction is to give him a fool for a companion. It is easy to find friends—of a sort; they freely offer to take you all about town; show you any place you wish to visit; you, of course, paying the expenses. The papers tell us about the confidence tricks played upon the verdant strangers, but they say nothing about the hundreds of city-bred young men, who ought to know better, who are yearly caught in the net of a poisonous friendship and are snared to their eternal ruin.

Beware, as for your life, of all companionships like these: the loafer; the gay Lothario; the skeptic; the untruthful man; the Sabbath-breaker; the profane swearer; the boaster of his wild deeds and vile associates; avoid, in short, every man whom you would not see seated in your own home shadow, sharing the unsuspected confidence of a father's, a mother's, or a sister's gentle love.

Remember that the assassin's dagger, driven into your mother's heart, would be a thousand times more merciful than the faintest whisper in your childhood's home of the story of your dissipation, your dishonesty, your intemperance, your impurity.

Hearts are the soul of honor—true friendship can be made only between true men. Elect as your friends your superiors, if possible; your equals, at least; your inferiors, never.

"Save me from my friends," is an old exclamation. The friend who led you into the abyss of sensuality or asked you to take the first drink has proven your enemy, and perhaps if he had blown your brains out he would have been a better friend. Alas! alas! for the direful contagion of evil companionship! Take counsel with wise and thoughtful men. Choose for your bosom friends men who will foster your piety and make you wiser, better and holier men. Lord Brooks was so proud of his friendship with Sir Philip Sydney that he chose for his epitaph: "Here lies Sir Philip Sydney's friend."

Choose friendships that are elevating. Walk not in the counsel of the ungodly; stand not in the way of sinners; sit not in the seat of the scornful; spend your evenings amid cheerful enjoyments, ennobling elevations and useful ameliorations.

Be it yours with the Psalmist to say, "I am a companion of them that fear thee, and of them that keep thy precepts."

XVIII.

ONLY those people who have investigated the subject have any idea of the enormity and magnitude of the vice of gambling, especially that form of gambling inseparably allied with race-tracks. The turf-gamblers have fastened themselves upon the necks of our courts, juries and legislatures. The proprietor of the most notorious race-track in New Jersey is the dictator of the State legislature, and this week had his "starter" elected speaker. The chief income of the racing associations is the money paid for gambling privileges, and so great is the income derived from this source that the stockholders of the racing associations become enormously wealthy, and the starters and jockeys are among the highest salaried men in the land. The vast sums of money required to maintain these associations come from the boys and young men who make up the multitude of the patrons of the pool-rooms. The prisons of New York and New

Jersey are full of young men who ascribe
their forgery, thefts and embezzlements to
their infatuation for pool-room gambling. No
form of gambling offers such temptations, and
the very fact that it requires so little money is
why the first theft from employers is so easily
made. Superintendent Byrnes says, " We are
sending men to prison right along on account
of the race-gambling craze."

I personally know of many homes that have
been destroyed and the lives of young men
blighted in the pool-rooms. I don't believe
that the cultivation of a horse's speed is a sin.
But the evil begins when the betting begins—
when fast horses make fast men. As horse-
racing is now conducted, race-tracks have become synonyms for all that is degrading in
modern life. It is time that the organized
gambling fraternity of the country be opposed
with an organized opposition—an opposition
that will expose the bought-and-sold legisla-
tors who curse the States of New York and
New Jersey. These pool-rooms are the snares
for our young men; they are the training-
schools of forgery and defalcation. Upon the
brow of every pool-seller I write the unmistak-
able word "Swindler." Let our cowardly, non-
committal, professedly Christian voters wake
up and send a cry to Albany for the repeal of

the Ives pool law. It is but self-defense to every banker who employs clerks, to every employer who intrusts money to other hands, to every father who has sons, to every man who loves righteousness, to join in the petition to our legislature to abolish the measure framed in the interest of vice and crime. Let the pulpits of New York and New Jersey blaze away at this, the greatest agency of vice and crime to-day, and let the people rise up and overthrow the turf-gambling monster.

XIX.

THIS united effort of all the churches, this virtuous outbreak against municipal corruption, this earnest endeavor to wipe away foul political stains from our fair escutcheon, is a grand display of patriotism. This conflict between the criminal classes on the one hand and the people on the other is a conflict as stern, and puts as severe a strain upon patriotism, as was ever endured upon the battlefield amid the glitter of cold steel and the rattle of musketry.

Thanks to the pulpit and the press, the rightful creators and conservators of public opinion, a flood of daylight has been thrown upon our city's government. The evil has been brought out. The monster has been dragged from his den for all New York to gaze at him, and hate him and kill him if they can.

The part of the ministers in politics is the patriotic spirit of the Roman. He was charged with violating the laws of his country. Fresh

109

from the fight, covered with the blood of a battlefield, where he had led his country's armies to victory, he replied, "I have broken the laws, but I have saved the State." And so the ministers of religion, throwing all the laws of spurious delicacy to the winds, will be able to say, "We have broken its laws, but we have saved the city from the panderers to vice, and successfully delivered the rising generation, who, all unconscious of their danger, are being caught in the mantraps of the city that now flourish either through municipal complicity or municipal stupidity."

As a rule, all our largest cities are the worst governed. Popular government in nearly all our cities has degenerated into a government by a "boss." Think of thousands of our citizens going to the polls led by a "boss"! Who is this "boss" whom the ambitious must court? Is he a man who earned the confidence of his fellow-men by the purity of his life, his integrity, competency and probity in public trusts, his deep study of the problems of government? In the light of notorious facts these questions sound satirical.

The city is a menace to our civilization, and as our cities grow larger and more dangerous the government will become more corrupt and control will pass into the hands of those who themselves most need to be controlled. It is the patriotic duty of every good citizen to be interested in municipal as well as State and national politics. No man can abjure politics and be either a good citizen or a good Christian.

It was one of the singular regulations of Solon, which declared a man dishonored and disfranchised who, in civil dispute, took no part with either side.

In the colonial days there were portions of New England in which votes were sent to householders, and if they did not use them they were fined.

The Greek word *idiot* is of Greek extraction, and meant with the Greeks a man who cared nothing for the public interest. Victor Hugo said, "Every honest man ought to be a politician." Charles Sumner often declared that "the citizen who neglects his political duties is a public enemy." Edmund Burke said, "When bad men combine the good must associate, else they will fall one by one an unpitied sacrifice in a contemptible struggle."

Every good man in politics wields a power for good. Every good man not in politics is to blame for political corruption, because by neglecting his plain duty he adds to the strength of the enemy. It behooves you as

Christians to realize that the good of humanity is bound up in the destiny of America, so as to carry it continually on your hearts and devoutly pray for it. It behooves you to lay hold of every privilege, with self-sacrificing patriotism to perform every duty of a citizen. Do not allow yourself to be driven by any party lash into a compromise of your convictions. Let it be known that with you principle amounts to something, that character counts, that transcendent party service cannot count upon your suffrage.

"The lewd fellows of the baser sort" have developed political trickery and corruption to the highest perfection in our cities, and the cities determine our State and national elections. Does not this fact contain an ominous augury for the future of our Republic? Unless there is an immediate grand rally of the good citizens, that will drive out of our politics these imported godless masses, sunk in ignorance, lost to the profession of religion, and even to the decent habits of civilized society, the prophecy that the ocean was dug for America's grave, that the winds were woven for her winding-sheet, and that the mountains were reared for her tombstone, will be fulfilled.

Matters are not so far gone but they may

be averted. A great French general who reached the battlefield at sundown and found that the troops of his country had been worsted in the fight, accosted the commander. Having rapidly learned how matters stood, he pulled out his watch, turned his eye on the sinking sun, and said, "There's yet time to gain the victory." He rallied the broken ranks. He placed himself at their head, and launching them with the arm of a giant in war upon the columns of the foe, snatched victory from the jaws of death. There is time yet also to save our city. But there is no time to lose. *There is no time to lose!*

XX.

In 1800 the Catholic population in the United States was 100,000. In 1890 it was 8,277,039. A fair estimate of the Catholic population of New York City is 750,000. A third of this number represents the Protestant church-going population of the city. In 1840 we had in this city one evangelical Protestant church to every 2071 of the population; in 1850, one to every 2442; in 1860, one to 2777; in 1870, one to 2480; in 1880, one to 3048; and in 1890, one to 3544, or if we take the police census, one to 4006. In comparison with the growth of the population, the Presbyterian Church has lost 17 per cent. in this city in twenty years. The Methodist Church in this city in nineteen years increased only 26½ per cent., and during the same time the population increased 80 per cent. The Dutch Reformed Church sustained a loss of 10 per cent., relative to the population. There is not a Protestant church in this city that has grown at all in proportion to the growth of the population.

The Christian forces at work below Fourteenth Street are not so large as they were twenty years ago, and although during that time 200,000 people have moved in below Fourteenth Street, twenty churches have moved out. One Jewish synagogue and two Catholic churches have been added, so that, counting churches of every kind, there are seventeen less than there were twenty years ago. Our pulpits ring with frequent appeals for money to establish missions in the destitute West. The population in the city of New York exceeds that of North and South Dakota, Montana, Washington, Oregon, Nevada, Colorado, and Wyoming. The Presbyterians and Congregationalists have only 85 pastors at work in this city, while in the States mentioned the two denominations have 540 pastors and workers.

The greatest mission field in America is in New York City, and not in the far regions. In the fourth and seventh wards of this city there are 70,000 people and seven Protestant churches and chapels. In the tenth ward there are 47,000 souls and two churches and one chapel. The twentieth ward increased 7¾ per cent. in population in ten years, and

its churches decreased 31 per cent. The drift
of our Protestant churches is always toward
the more fashionable parts of the city. The
magnificent churches built up-town have not
been built by the people, but the money came
from the sale of down-town churches, where
hundreds of thousands of dollars were often
realized for the ground, and churches left
behind chapels for the poor on back streets.
The Protestant church deserves to fail, so
long as, in defiance of the Christ spirit, it
builds fine churches for the few and pauper-
izes the poor by building plain chapels for
them. God's house should be built for all
alike.

"The churches must follow the people" is
the cry. Who are the people? The up-town
rich and fashionables, where the churches all
seem anxious to crowd and hinder each other's
growth by ruinous rivalry? Only a few days
ago the New York Presbytery advised two
down-town congregations to dissolve their
organizations and sell their churches, so that
the money might be used in removing the
indebtedness of fashionable up-town churches.
We have systematically robbed the down-town
poor by selling their churches to get money
to build churches for the rich few.

The Catholic Church never surrenders an

old field; none of her churches is ever turned into secular uses. The people must build their own churches. To what, then, is the Catholic Church indebted for its triumphant march? To the monstrosity of our frequent moving days, the indifference of Protestants, and the enthusiasm of Catholics. It is because the Catholics are thoroughly devoted and in earnest, and are prepared to make sacrifices and to suffer in order to support what they believe to be true.

XXI.

LET NOT YOUR ANGRY PASSIONS RISE.

WHEN the storm of passion has cleared away the angry man sees that he has been a fool, and he has made himself a fool in the eyes of others too. Getting "mad" never helps matters. No man ever got along better for getting angry. To be angry with a weak man proves that you are not very strong yourself. "Anger," says Pythagoras, "begins with folly and ends with repentance."

Many men otherwise very good have allowed a bad temper to get the mastery over them so as to make themselves and those about them very uncomfortable. A minister was dressing himself one day so as to go out and make pastoral calls. But when he came to fix the collar round his neck he found that the button was gone from his shirt and he could not fasten the collar. All at once his patience left him. He began to storm and used unkind words about it, so that his wife burst into tears, hastened to her room, sat down, and had a good cry.

When the minister got through with his dressing he went out to make his calls. He first called on an old man who was suffering greatly from rheumatism and was unable to use his limbs. But he found him patient and even cheerful. Then he called on a young man who was wasting away with consumption and expecting soon to die. But he had a hope in Christ. He could sing:

> "The world recedes, it disappears,
> Heaven opens on my eyes, my ears
>   With sounds seraphic ring.
> Lend, lend your wings, I mount, I fly—
> O grave, where is thy victory!
> O Death, where is thy sting!"

Then he called on an old grandmother, who lived all by herself in a miserable old garret. As he was going upstairs into her forlorn chamber he heard her cheerful voice singing:

> "There is a land of pure delight,
>   Where saints immortal reign;
> Eternal day excludes the night,
>   And pleasures banish pain."

Lying on her hard pallet, by her side were a crust of bread and a cup of cold water, and an open Bible with the passage marked: *"The foxes have holes, and the birds of the air have nests, but the son of man has not where to lay his head."* And she said, "O blessed Bible!

It is as if a shining angel talked to me out of
heaven. My poor chamber seems heaven's
gate, and I am happy—so happy!" The last
call he made was at a home of sorrowing love.
A young mother sat by the coffin of her first-
born child. Her cheeks were stained with
tears. She had been pressing her lips to that
cold forehead and twining her fingers in that
silken hair. But to his surprise she was cheerful. She said, "My Saviour said, 'Suffer little children to come unto me, and forbid them
not, for of such is the kingdom of heaven!'
My babe has gone to heaven; my lamb is in
the Shepherd's bosom."

The minister went home at the close of that
afternoon feeling very thankful for all that he
had seen, and deeply impressed with the pre-
cious comforting of Christ. In the evening he
was sitting in his easy-chair before the fire, and
his wife sat near him, busy with her needle.
In thinking of the visits he had made to those
different homes of affliction he could not help
saying, "What a wonderful thing the grace
of God is! How much it can do! Nothing
is too hard for it. Wonderful! wonderful!
It can do all things."

"Yes, it is wonderful indeed," said his little
wife; "and yet there is *one thing* which the
grace of God does not seem to have power to do."

"And pray what can that be?" asked her husband.

"Why, it does not seem to have power to control a minister's temper when he finds that his shirt button is gone." In a moment the minister's conscience smote him. He saw what a sin he had committed in giving way to an angry temper, and how that anger had interfered with the happiness of his family. With his eyes full of tears he said, "Forgive me, my dear wife, for the wrong I have done. I will ask God that I may never give way to such an angry temper again."

XXII.

IS THERE A HELL?

Is there a hell, or is all that we are told about it the creation of superstitious fears? If we trace the history of this belief we shall find that it has not been entertained by superstitious people alone, but by the wisest and best men of every age—heathens as well as Jews and Christians—and this fact ought of itself shake the unbelief of the most intelligent skeptic. If the wisest and best men of every age, with all their differences of opinion upon other points, have unanimously agreed in the belief of a future state of retribution, this fact claims every man's respectful attention, and no man who wishes to have credit for good common sense will say that the belief in a hell is nothing more than a superstition or an invention of priestcraft for making an easy livelihood. The question, Is there a hell? resolves itself into this: Is there a moral governor of the world? Is there a moral law? Is there such a thing as sin?

For if there be, then there is such a thing as punishment for sin, and that punishment, whatever form it may assume, may be designated hell.

But are not all men punished for their sins in this life? We see every day that there is not for all sin such a reckoning in this world as meets the claims of righteousness and justice. There are many whose evil doings pass undetected and unpunished, whom neither the laws of man nor the laws of nature can reach. Thousands of the greatest criminals have gone to their graves in peace. Death had no revenging terrors, no retributive remorse for them. And when we take a deliberate view and see how the righteous often suffer and the wicked flourish, we are naturally led to exclaim, "Wherefore do the wicked live, become old; yea, are mighty in power? Is there no reward for the righteous? Is there no punishment for the workers of iniquity? Is there no God that judgeth on the earth?" And, indeed, were there no retributions beyond the limits of this present life we should be necessarily obliged to admit one or the other of the following conclusions: Either that no moral governor of the world exists, or that justice and judgment are not the habitation of his throne.

How can you have a heaven without a hell? For if there be no hell then all must go to heaven. But you can no more have a heaven without a hell than you can have a pure and clean city, free from nuisance and pestilence, without scavengers, sewers and sinks. A pure city implies impure commons, where all that is unfit to be in the city is cast out. The wicked surely cannot be with the saints; they must be together by themselves where the unholy passions that reign in them would soon make a hell. If there be no future punishment, if all go to heaven when they die, then a rope will do more for a man and transfer him quicker to heaven than a life-long service for Christ. Vice is connived at and virtue discouraged if there be no future retribution. If there is no retribution, then we must expect to have for our immortal associates drunkards, blasphemers and all the base villains that ever disgraced humanity. No hell is contradictory to conscience and reason. The future punishment of the impenitent wicked is what our common sense demands.

XXIII.

Much has been said and written of the New York tenement houses, their gloom, filth and squalor, of the cruel landlordism, and I know from personal investigations that the wretchedness in which thousands of our unfortunate brothers and sisters live has not been overdrawn. The most skilled artist would find his pencil lie broken before him if he attempted to delineate upon canvas the wretchedness of the slums. The most acute conception of the reporter's fancy, the most graphic description of the orator, the boldest flights of the poet's imagination, would be inadequate in executing a descriptive scene of the woes of our poor and our abominable landlordism.

These tenements are not only the nurseries of seventy-five per cent. of our crime, but they are also the abodes of many worthy poor who are struggling against their surroundings to improve their condition, and give their children a better chance in the race of life than they themselves had.

The death-rate in Hester Street is forty per cent. higher than the average made by the plague in Brazil, and throughout the tenement district the deaths usually outnumber the births, so that if it were not for the continued stream of immigration the tenement house problem would soon solve itself.

The vast majority of our down-town and east-side tenements are not fit to be inhabited; the landlords do not pretend to obey the laws of health, yet the tenants are paying large enough rents to yield landlords and estates from ten to twenty per cent. A recent writer in *The Forum* says: "One man boasted that he draws thirty-three per cent. on his tenement investments." Rear lofts and sub-cellars rent from $1.50 to $4.00 a week. Talk of evictions in Ireland, they are nothing compared to the evictions and cruel landlordism of our slums!

The landlord is often an enormously wealthy estate which hires an agent, whose only business is to show a large balance of profits, and the poorer the tenements the larger the profits. O landlord or estate too busy to collect your own rents, it is your duty to glorify God in your property as well as in your body and soul; it is for you to *know how* your agent can bring you from fifteen to

twenty per cent. profit on your tenement investments. The enormous sums that our
wretched poor pay for the most wretched ac-
commodations seem so incredible that I hesitate to present figures.

Our large moneyed institutions which find
it difficult to secure safe investments at four
per cent. should take hold of this tenement
question. Philanthropists with big bank ac-
counts should look in this direction as a field
in which to uplift their fellow-men. There is
a greater demand for this class of benevolent
investments in New York than there is for
added cathedrals, churches, colleges or charity
organizations. The greatest benefaction that
could befall this city would be the replacing
of our tenements by such buildings as the
Victoria Square in Liverpool. On this square
once stood miserable tenement houses. To-
day a magnificent structure stands there, built
around a hollow square, a large portion of
which is given up to a playground for the
children. All arrangements in the house are
according to the demands of modern science.
No room is smaller than thirteen by eighteen
feet and six inches; the ceilings are nine feet
high. Three-room tenements rent for $1.44 a
week, while one-room quarters are let at 54
cents a week. The total expenditure on the

building was $338,000, and though built as
a philanthropic enterprise the returns are estimated at four and a half per cent. Who
among the many millionaires of this city will
lead off in some such crusade that will give
to our worthy poor healthier and cleaner
shelter?

XXIV.

THIS war upon our Sabbath is a foreign war. Will you give up the American Sabbath bequeathed to you by your fathers? What have you to say to the transatlantic comers who propose to Europeanize America? Are you cowardly enough to sit in sackcloth and ashes before the enemies of God while they impudently strike at our most sacred institution? Will you not defend it as long as there is any strength in your arm or blood in your heart?

> "Woodman, spare that tree!
> Touch not a single bough!
> In youth it sheltered me,
> And I'll protect it now."

If foreigners will not assimilate with us as American citizens, if they do not admire our Sabbath and Christian institutions, if they want social incendiarism and sabbatic disorder, a go-as-you-please Sabbath, they are welcome to enjoy it—by recrossing the Atlantic—the sooner the better, and that, too, with our warmest benedictions! But if they stay here, we demand the enforcement of that central truth of statecraft—the liberty of the individual subject to the sovereignty of the State—the subordination of individual rights and privileges to the general good; these are integral elements in a stable national life. Bartholdi's Statue of Liberty on Bedloe's Island, opposite Castle Garden, holding in her right hand a torch, should hold in her left hand a volume containing the laws and customs of the land, and before the right hand be extended in welcome, require upon bended knee the left hand to be kissed as a token of submission to our laws, customs and institutions.

This secularization of the Sabbath is a plain violation of the statutes of our State. Every Sabbath-breaker is a criminal, and he who attempts to override the laws of the State insults every American citizen.

It is a war upon our political institutions. In countries where the Sabbath is most profaned, like Spain, France, Italy and Bavaria, society is grossly immoral. In Sabbath-observing England, Scotland and America, society is found in its highest moral tone. Pick out the hamlets or cities, or wards of cities, where are the lowest moral conditions, and there just in proportion is the Sabbath desecrated. An eminent judge of the United States Supreme Court forcibly said: "Where there is no Christian Sabbath there is no Christian morality; and without this free government cannot be maintained." Blackstone says: "The Sabbath is of admirable service to the State, considered merely as a civil institution."

History's lesson is that morality and Sabbath-keeping walk hand in hand in inseparable affinity. Society is degraded as Christianity is corrupted; and Christianity is vitiated as the Sabbath is perverted. History most clearly proves that every nation and community has been prospered while it honored God's Sabbath, and that social order and the supremacy of the law have not been maintained where the Sabbath has been trampled on. Look abroad over the map of popular freedom in the world—Switzerland, Scotland, England and the United States, the countries which best observe the Sabbath, constitute almost the entire map of safe popular government.

Some years ago, De Tocqueville, the distinguished French statesman, was commissioned by his country for the purpose of studying the genius of our institutions. In reporting to the French Senate, he said: "I went at your bidding, and passed along their thoroughfares of trade. I ascended their mountains, and went down their valleys. I visited their manufactories, their commercial markets and emporiums of trade. I entered their judicial courts and legislative halls. But I sought everywhere in vain for the secret of their success, until I entered the church. It was there, as I listened to the soul-equalizing and soul-elevating principles of the Gospel of Christ, as they fell from Sabbath to Sabbath upon the masses of the people, that I learned why America was great and free, and why France was a slave."

In the dark days of the French Revolution, "the shabbiest page of human annals," as Carlyle calls it, the Sabbath was trampled in the dust, and a tenth day of rest substituted without divine sanction; and so frightful did society become that the infidel authorities had to institute the holy Sabbath and public worship to save the metropolis and the country from utter desolation. France is yet reaping the sad fruitage of her folly, and she will never have a permanent republic until she quits her roaring, roystering and rollicking Sabbaths and devotes one day in every week to the recognition of God.

I believe that the security or disaster of American institutions depends upon the issue of the Sabbath contest. The end of the Sabbath would be for the United States the beginning of the reign of Mammon, Bacchus and Venus, and finally overwhelm us in temporal and eternal ruin. From such a fate may the God of Lexington and Gettysburg deliver us!

The Sabbath question is a question of life and death in regard to Christianity. The enemies of religion tried the sword and the fagot. They could not destroy the Gospel. Imperial power found its arm too weak to contend with God. Argument, ridicule and sophistry were all in vain. Christianity rose with augmented power and more resplendent beauty. The last weapon the enemy seeks to employ to destroy Christianity is to corrupt the Sabbath and make it a day of festivity. Voltaire truly said: "There is no hope of destroying Christianity so long as the Sabbath is kept as a sacred day." Dr. Philip Schaff says: "The Sabbath is the strongest bond that binds the different Protestant denominations." I congratulate our city that notwithstanding the complex character of our population we have escaped the invasion so well. But I call upon all Christian citizens

and lovers of political freedom to stand unanimously and irresistibly in this Thermopylæ
of our American history. Declare before high
heaven that you will not give up the Sabbath,
and that you will bring ignominious defeat to
the enemies of God and the public weal!

XXV.

THE greatest waste of life is wasted or perverted power. How few men make their lives noble! They sink into the grave with scarcely a trace to indicate that they ever lived. They lived and they died. Cradle and grave are closely brought together; there is nothing between them. There have been hundreds who could have rivaled the patriotism of a Washington, or the humanity of a Howard, or the eloquence of a Demosthenes, and who have left behind them no one memorial of their existence, because of lack of lofty courage, sublime moral heroism, the assertion of individuality. The world's great things have been accomplished by individuals. Vast social reformations have originated in individual souls. Truths that now sway the world were first proclaimed by individual lips. Great thoughts that are now the axioms of humanity proceeded from the center of individual hearts. Let not others fashion what your life shall be. Thomas Carlyle says that he would like to stop the stream of people in the Strand and ask every man his history. "But no," says the sage, "I will not stop them. If I did I should find they were like a flock of sheep following in the track of one another."

Alas! men begin to lose their individuality of conviction the moment they begin life's business. Many a young man has sacrificed his individuality on the altar that a profligate companion built for him. Many a young man who knew right has allowed some empty-headed street-corner loafer to lower his own high moral tone lest he should seem singular in the little world of society surrounding him.

Thousands become bad, not because they intended to be bad, but because they had not the courage to resolve to do good.

The worst weakness in the world is to fear to do right because others will criticise it. Dare to be singular! Dare to stand alone and unflinchingly for the right, though the earth reels and the heavens fall!

I don't disparage associations. Exaggerated individuality makes a man impracticable. But the danger of our times is to shape ourselves by others, so as to destroy force and effectiveness, to think in cliques.

Live, then, like an individual. Take life

like a man—as though the world had waited for your coming. Don't take your cue from other men—the weak, the prejudiced, the trimmers, the cowards—but rather from the illustrious ones of earth. Dare to take the side that seems wrong to man's blinded eye. Scorn the praise of men. Learn to live with God, and you will pass from manhood to immortality with the seal of God upon your brow.

XXVI.

GAMBLERS AND GAMBLING.

I SOLEMNLY warn you against gambling, because:

1. It is illegal. No man ever gambles but is a criminal to the law of God and to the law of the land.

2. It is dishonest. It is taking that to which you have no claim. Hazard is no title; winning is no ownership. Only fair exchange is no robbery.

3. It is destructive. Gamblers are seldom industrious men in any useful vocation. Labor loses its relish as the passion for play increases. It destroys all domestic habits and affections. The gambler may for a moment sport with his children and smile upon his wife, but his heart is not at home. "A little branch rill may flow through the family, but the deep well of his affections flows away from home." It destroys all that is good in the soul, vitiates the whole character, and drags down every lofty purpose and noble inspiration. Once in the fatal snare,

the gambler is seldom saved. Friends may warn, the wife entreat with the eloquence of her tears, and children cry for bread, but deaf as the adder, desperate as the maniac, he rushes on, regardless of danger, reckless of consequences.

4. It is a poor business. All the odds are against you. You have ten chances to be struck with lightning to one for winning. Men go in for wool and come out shorn. Every gambler sooner or later goes to the dogs.

5. It is an unhappy business. The gloomiest set of men in the world are your betting men. They are always on the edge of a precipice. They are in perpetual danger of being reduced to beggary.

6. It ruins at last. You may gain all that the tables of earth can bear, but it may be the price of a lost soul. The devil, the arch-gambler, is cunningly playing for your soul. Life is a mighty game, in which you are the stake. Who shall be the winner—God or the devil?

XXVII.

WANTED—HONEST MEN.

I AM not one of those who believe that "every man has his price," and that "an honest man has a lock of hair growing in the palm of his right hand." No! There are in the world of business many more honest men than rogues, and for one trust betrayed there are thousands most sacredly kept. I have no sympathy with the cynic who, as history informs us, being ordered to summon the good men of the city before the Roman censor, proceeded immediately to the graveyard, and, standing on a grave, called to the dead below, saying he knew not where to find a good man alive; or that sour sage, that prince of gamblers, who could speak in praise of no one but himself and his wife (the latter deserving all the praise she got for enduring him so long), I refer to Thomas Carlyle, who described the population of his country as consisting of so many millions, "mostly fools." When any one complains, as Diogenes did, that he has to hunt the streets with candles at noonday to find an honest man, we are apt to think that his nearest neighbor would have quite as much difficulty in making such a discovery. If you think there is not a true man living you had better, for appearance's sake, not say so until you are dead yourself.

But some of the most gigantic scoundrels have fattened on sermons about love, faith, inspiration, the efficacy of the sacraments, and heaven, who ought by practical preaching to have been thundered out of the church, where their presence was a sacrilege and a disgrace. Mr. Froude, the distinguished English historian and essayist, said that he had heard hundreds of sermons on the non-essentials, "but never, during these thirty wonderful years, never one, that I can recollect, on common honesty, or those primitive commandments—thou shalt not lie; thou shalt not steal."

The bankrupt laws of our land have reduced stealing to a fine art. Our laws are making people dishonest by fixing it so that a man can wipe out his debts by compromising with his creditors.

"The world is a goose, to succeed you must pick
The feathers off nicely by buying on tick;
The vulgar pickpocket is sent off to jail;
Be polite; give your note, and gracefully fail."

Strange, but true, a man will be treated
kindly in proportion to the severity of his fall.
Smash on a small scale, and the world will
jump on you with both feet; smash on a
grand scale, and the world will take you by
the hand. What the world needs more than
anything else right now is downright honesty,
and the church will never convert the world
until she gets honest. She has too many
members who are agents for and boarders with
their wives. A man's church-membership has
not the commercial value of one dollar. There
are thousands of men in our churches who do
not tell the truth. I was reading the other
day of an old Hard-Shell Baptist down in
Georgia who walked into a store one day and
said to the merchant, "I want a couple of
hundred dollars' worth of goods this year on
credit." The merchant looked at his old hat
and jean pants, and concluded that he was
not the sort of man to trust, and he told him
he would not give him the goods. The man
walked out, and the merchant asked the clerk
in the store, "Who is that man?" "That's
Mr. So-and-so, and he belongs to the Hard-
Shell church up here." The merchant went
out after him and said, "Friend, come back
here. Are you a Hard-Shell?" He said,
"Yes." "Well," said the merchant, "you can

have all you want; you can have all here in this store on credit for as long time as you need." And down in Georgia the Hard-Shells will turn defaulters out of church just as quickly as they will drunkards. I hope to see the day when you may sell the last thing a man has who *can* but won't pay his honest debts. How can you keep the things that the people ought to have? If all our church members would pay their debts the world would have more confidence in the church and in Christianity.

As a mere matter of selfishness, "honesty is the best policy." But he who is honest for policy's sake is already a moral bankrupt. Men of policy are conscientiously (?) honest when they think honesty will pay the better, but when policy will pay better they give honesty the slip. Honesty and policy have nothing in common. When policy is in, honesty is out. It is more honorable for some men to fail than for others to succeed. Rather be like Longfellow's honest blacksmith, "who looked the whole world in the face and feared not any man," than enrich yourself at the sacrifice of conscience and the blessing of Heaven.

Part with anything rather than your integrity and conscious rectitude. Capital is not

what a man has, but what a man is. Character is capital.

"Take thou no thought for aught save truth and right,
  Content if such thy fate to die obscure;
Wealth palls, and honors, fame may not endure,
  And loftier souls soon weary of delight.

"Keep innocence, be all a true man ought,
  Let neither pleasures tempt nor pain appall;
Who hath this, he hath all things, having naught;
  Who hath it not, hath nothing, having all."

XXVIII.

Byron in "Don Juan" says, "Sweet is revenge." But we rather agree with Milton:

> "Revenge at first though sweet,
> Bitter ere long, back on itself recoils."

Juvenal says, "Revenge is only the pleasure
of a little, weak and narrow mind." Lord
Karnes truly says, " The indulgence of revenge
tends to make men more savage and cruel."
The dog believes that revenge is sweet, and
with almost human tenacity cherishes ideas
of revenge. The length of time a dog will
treasure up the remembrance of an injury is
truly marvelous. "He forgets neither friend
nor foe," says Sir Walter Scott, "remembers,
and with accuracy, both benefit and injury."
In his delightful "Anecdotes of Dogs," Jesse
furnishes some noteworthy instances of this
strength of canine memory. On one occasion,
according to his story, a traveler, in passing

145

on horseback through a small Cumberland village, out of pure thoughtlessness struck with his whip at a large Newfoundland dog that reposed by the wayside. The enraged animal rushed at him and pursued him for a considerable distance. One year later his business took him to the same village, and as he was leading his horse, the dog, recollecting him, seized his leg, the teeth penetrating through the boot, and the animal might have done him serious injury had not assistance been procured. Revenge is not *manhood*, it is rather *doghood*. The manlier any man is, the milder and more merciful will he be; as Julius Cæsar, who, when he had Pompey's head presented to him, wept and said, "I seek not revenge, but victory."

When you are tempted to give the cutting word, or hasty answer, check yourself with the question: Is this the reply my Saviour would have given? If your fellow-men should prove unkind, inconsiderate and ungrateful, be it yours to refer the cause to God. *Revenge!* No such word should have a place in the Christian's vocabulary. *Revenge!* If I cherish such a feeling toward my brother, how can I meet that brother in heaven? Christ did not answer cutting taunts and unmerited wrong. "Who, when he was reviled, reviled not again."

"Let this mind be in you which was also in Christ Jesus." "Overcome evil with good." Don't be irritable, huffy, sensitive. Don't lose your temper. Don't lose it, did I say? Lose it, by all means. If a man is as jealous, passionate, huffy, sullen, sour, moody, miffy and revengeful after his conversion as he was before it, what is he converted from or to? We live only by the forbearance of God. We are to repeat in our lives to others at least something of His patience towards us. We are taught to pray every day: "Forgive us our debts, *as we forgive* our debtors." If we are exacting and revengeful, if we cannot forgive the unkind treatment of others, how can we sincerely pray this petition? The sweetest revenge is to forgive and forget.

"Let by-gones be by-gones; if by-gones were clouded
    By aught that occasioned a pang of regret,
Oh, let them in darkest oblivion be shrouded,
    'Tis wise and 'tis kind to forgive and forget.

"Let by-gones be by-gones and good be extracted
    From ill over which it is folly to fret;
The wisest of mortals have foolishly acted—
    The kindest are those who forgive and forget.

"Let by-gones be by-gones; oh, cherish no longer
    The thought that the sun of affection has set;
Eclipsed for a moment its rays will be stronger
    If you, like a Christian, forgive and forget.

"Let by-gones be by-gones; your heart will be lighter
  When kindness of yours with reception has met.
The flame of your heart will be purer and brighter
  If God-like, you strive to forgive and forget.

"Let by-gones be by-gones; oh, purge out the leaven
  Of malice, and try an example to set
To others, who, craving the mercy of Heaven
  Are sadly too slow to forgive and forget.

"Let by-gones be by-gones; remember how deeply
  To Heaven's forbearance we all are in debt!
They value God's infinite goodness too cheaply
  Who heed not the precept 'Forgive and forget.'"

XXIX.

THERE has recently been formed in this city a "Burial Reform Association," the principal aims of which are to secure simple funeral services, to promote inexpensive funerals, to discourage excessive display of flowers, the wearing of crape, especially of crape veils, which if worn over the head not only disguise the wearer, but put the eyes to a severe strain to look through its black meshes, and if worn thrown back pull so upon the hair that it is not uncommon for the wearer to suffer severely.

Dark colors, even black, may be appropriately worn, but crape calls attention to the person in mourning, and you can almost detect for whom the mourning is, and often the length of time it has been going on—all of which is a satire on real grief, which mourns in secret.

Paul's glad victory over death and the grave is muffled by the raven feathers of funereal plumes. The waving crape upon the doorknob; the darkened windows; the body shrouded and coffined in the color of gloom; women and children veiled and draped in dispiriting black; men's hats banded with crape —what hopelessness all these things express! They symbolize doubt, despair, agony and gloom. They express no Christian comfort, breathe no heavenly consolation, suggest no immortal hope, inspire no sure confidence. I have seen the ultra-fashionable cover their pet dogs with crape, and crape-mounted horses, coachmen and footmen are used to further emphasize these negations of Christian truth.

We have "full mourning," "mourning jewelry," "mourning visiting-cards," "mourning stationery," which by its gradual narrowing indicates that the days of mourning are approaching their end; but the ghastly humor of our mourning customs reaches its climax in "second mourning," followed by the full bloom of gorgeous colors, for the time appointed by the inexorable decree of fashionable society has passed, and now mourning may be laid aside with funereal garments.

If you depreciate these practices, when death occurs in your family have the courage to do away with what good sense declares objectionable features. Dare to defy silly social customs.

Take the matter of flowers. In many households there is a display offensive to refined taste, and among the poor the display is frequently sinful in its profusion; they put their last dollar into flowers. Funerals are nowadays so expensive that it costs more to die than to live. I have known men who died solvent but became insolvent before they got under the ground. Our undertakers are frequently swindled. It is not only false reverence and mistaken affection, but downright dishonesty, if a man's family or friends indulge expenditures that cannot be met.

Take the matter of funeral addresses. Generally the less good a man has done the more good the preacher is expected to say of him, and the preachers often discharge their duty in this particular in such a way as to bring their profession into ridicule.

To hold the funerals of haters of churches in the church is trying to do for their bodies what they would never do for their souls. It seems like taking a mean advantage of a man after he is dead, to take him by force where he could not be persuaded to go when he was alive. The most sacred place in which to hold the funeral service is the quiet home.

Sunday funerals are rarely necessary; they nearly always assume a magnitude that amounts to Sabbath desecration. The Lord's day is for rest and divine worship, and not for great funeral pageants.

XXX. .

DANCING.

Dancing in proper forms is healthy; it improves the bearing of our youth, tends to relieve their natural awkwardness in society, and is innocent. An amiable clergyman happened to be present one evening when some young ladies went through a quadrille. He looked on with great pleasure. The next morning he was called to account by some of his busy neighbors for having, by his presence, countenanced dancing. He emphatically denied the charge, and asserted that no dancing had taken place, but only, as he expressed it, *" a most beautiful exercise."* If stepping to music is innocent, I cannot see how skipping to music can be converted into sin. For one I am glad that nearly all the Christian families of the highest standing in all of our churches have asserted their right to act out their own convictions in this matter, and have shown that this much berated amusement can be elevated and refined. I am not a preacher of gloom, but of moderation. Harmless things may become sinful by excess.

Dancing frequently leads to the sacrifice of health. The physical education of women is at the best too much disregarded in this country. Woman's dress is arranged with regard to looks rather than health. How small is the number of healthy women in the higher classes of society! How pale and languid are the young women when winter is over! Many of them look as if they had just recovered from a long illness. The objections I have to the dance are found in the excessive exercise in a heated and overcrowded room, in the late hours, insufficient apparel, in extravagance and gormandish indulgence at the supper-table. Remove or moderate these things, bring this amusement within the bounds of reason, and no sensible man will find fault. Instead of imitating the foolish customs of European society, let good sense—for the sake of novelty, if for nothing else—become fashionable. The dance takes too great a place and occupies too much time in modern society; it effectually stops intellectual improvement, and crowds out intelligent conversation. Conversation is one of the lost arts. Good talkers are almost extinct creatures. Many people's talk is merely an exercise of the tongue. No other human faculty has any share in it. Many men and women are educated failures. It is not enough for women to sit stiff and look wise through double-extra eyeglasses. They are oppressive. If at an evening party you should retire to a corner of the room and note the talk of the company and produce a verbatim report of the conversation, each speaker would feel lamentably chagrined at the superficial and trifling character of his or her utterances. It is a common saying, that it is not half so bad to dance at an evening party as it is to be in another room and slander your neighbors. The members of my church are not obliged to do either. Avoid personalities in your conversation. Talk about things instead of conversing about people. People who read and think converse about ideas and things. Of the virtuous woman Solomon says: "She openeth her mouth with wisdom, and in her tongue is the law of kindness."

> "Nay, speak no ill; a kindly word
> Can never leave a sting behind;
> And oh, to breathe each tale we've heard
> Is far beneath a noble mind."

XXXI.

ALL the medical fraternities of the United States and Great Britain, allopathic, homœopathic, hydropathic, eclectic and electric, condemn cigarette smoking as one of the most destructive evils that ever befell the youth of any country, declaring that its direct tendency is a deterioration of the race. The cigarette is overshadowing every other branch of the tobacco business. It is estimated that seven hundred millions of cigarettes are manufactured annually in our country. Investigation has shown that cigarettes, as a rule, are adulterated, and more injurious than tobacco. A physician had a cigarette analyzed, and found the tobacco to be strongly impregnated with opium, while the wrapper, warranted to be rice-paper, proved to be common paper whitened with arsenic. An eminent physician pronounces cigarettes to be worse for boys than cigars, because the paper absorbs more of the nicotine. Nicotine is one of the subtlest of poisons. Brodie, Queen Victoria's physician, made several experiments with nicotine, applying it to the tongues of a mouse, a squirrel and a dog. Death was produced in every instance. Hold white paper over the smoke of a cigarette, scrape the condensed smoke from the paper, and put a small quantity on the tongue of a cat, and in spite of its " nine lives " it will instantly writhe in convulsions and die. Dr. Hammond gives it as his testimony that " no speedier method for rendering existence painful is more efficacious than to smoke cigarettes and to inhale the fumes into the lungs. By this practice a very large absorbing surface is exposed to the action of the nicotine and other poisonous products which are evolved when tobacco is burned. As a consequence the system is more thoroughly subjected to their influence and disease more certainly produced. The action of the brain is impaired thereby, the ability to think, and in fact all mental concentration are weakened. Neuralgia, especially about the face, throat diseases, nasal catarrh, serious affections of the eyes, dyspepsia, and, above all, interruption in the normal action of the heart, are among the consequences resulting from the inhalation of cigarette smoke."

A distinguished French physician has investigated the effect of smoking on thirty-eight boys, between the ages of nine and fifteen, who were addicted to the habit. Twenty-seven presented distinct symptoms of nicotine poison. In 22 there were serious disorders of the circulation, indigestion, dullness of intellect, and a marked appetite for strong drink. In 3 there was heart affection, in 8 decided deterioration of blood. In 12 there was frequent bleeding of the nose; 10 had disturbed sleep, and 4 had ulceration of the mouth.

Tobacco attacks the nervous system and thereby impairs the mental faculties. Dr. Willard Parker says: "Tobacco is ruinous in our schools, dwarfing the body and mind." At an examination for admission to the Free College of New York, out of 900 girls, 660, or 71 per cent., passed, while only 48 per cent. of the boys could enter, the difference being ascribed to the stupefying effects of tobacco. The effect of tobacco on schoolboys is so marked as not to be open for discussion. The classes of Yale are graded according to their scholarship. In the first division only 25 per cent. use tobacco; in the second, 48; in the third, 70; and in the lowest, 85. During the last fifty years no devotee of the weed has graduated from Harvard at the head of his class, although above 83 per cent. of the students are addicted to its use.

There are in this city a good many "cigar-butt grubbers," as they are termed; that is, boys and girls who scour the streets for stumps and half-burnt cigars, which are dried and then sold to be used in making cigarettes. A ragged eight-year-old Italian boy, bareheaded and barefooted, was brought before one of the city justices on the charge of vagrancy. The officer who arrested him stated that he found the boy picking up cigar stumps from the streets and gutters, showing the justice a basket half-full of such stumps, water-soaked, and covered with mud. "What do you do with these?" asked his Honor. "I sell them to a man for ten cents a pound, and they are used for making cigarettes." A Southern tobacconist stated to a New York *Tribune* representative that the extent to which drugs are used in cigarettes is appalling, and that "Havana flavoring" is sold by the thousand barrels, prepared from the tonka-bean, which contains a deadly poison. Cigar wrappers in many cases are made from the filthy scrapings of rag-pickers, arsenic being often used in the bleaching process, while combustion develops the oil of creosote.

Boys, would you have your bodily powers developed; would you be strong, vigorous-minded men? Don't smoke! On our streets we behold a vast and ever-increasing number of boys who evidently consider smoking essential to manliness. And our police have orders to stop all boys under sixteen! Parents are surprisingly ignorant of the habits of their boys in this regard, and when not ignorant, surprisingly timid and criminally indifferent. Would to God that all fathers were models to their boys.

Boys, break away now, before you are bound hand and foot to a pitiable thralldom. Think of a *man* mastered by a *cigarette!*

XXXII.

THE BRIDAL SCENE AT CANA.

THIS wedding, made forever the most memorable one in history by the presence and grace of Christ, was celebrated in the lovely little town of Cana, three miles northeast of Nazareth, " lying in the lap of the Galilean hills like a bird in its nest."

There is something significant in the fact that the Saviour began his miracles at a wedding rather than at a funeral—the grave of Lazarus, or the gate of Nain. It was a practical reproof of the asceticism that scorns the happiness of social and domestic affections, and that would make of life a ghostly austerity, just as if men were heavenly because they were unearthly.

No personal act more deeply involves happiness than marriage. Yet the general conversation on this ordinance is lamentably below the high standard God has given to it. Marriage is the perfected life of love between two kindred spirits; and yet how often it is merely a society affair between two exquisite fools;

matrimony is made a *matter-of-money*, and how often the lips utter vows of love which the heart can never ratify. A marriage for anything but love is a humiliating stoop to the dust, a mockery that blushes to the skies. Love is founded upon esteem, and is therefore under the control of reason.

Marry "only in the Lord." "For how can two walk together except they be agreed?" If there is one place at which husband and wife should meet in the completest harmony, it is at the cross of Christ.

> "Together should their prayers ascend,
> Together should they humbly bend
> To praise the Almighty name."

Those who are one in Christ fight double-handed against evil. The child of God will bring a blessing to your house above earthly riches.

Make Christ one of your wedding-guests. Never should the duty with the prayer, "Commit thy way unto him, and he will direct thy paths," be more intensely realized than at the marriage altar. With your selected and future companion say to him, "If *thy presence* go not with us, carry us not up hence." If earnestly solicited by you, Christ will now, as of old, by his presence beautify and bless your bridal

hour, sanctify your joy, and leave his bene-
diction upon your hearts to perpetuate your
love, and fulfill all the happy prophecies of the
bridal day. Without the presence of Christ
to bless the marriage, the congratulations and
good wishes of friends will be only empty
words, the flowers will wither and the music
grow discordant.

Having entered upon your new home, get
down upon your knees together, and ask Christ
to consecrate it. The faith of heart in heart
will die without faith in Christ. Love puri-
fied by religion is the fragrant blossom that
will gladden the heart and beautify the hum-
blest home.

> "Home's not merely four square walls,
>   Though with pictures hung and gilded;
>   Home is where affection calls,
>   Filled with shrines the heart hath builded."

This sanctified love instantly recalls the
hasty word; it stands upon no dignity as to
whose place it is to yield first to the other;
it lets not the sun go down upon an angry
thought or feeling between two hearts that
have been made one. It transforms blemishes
into imaginary virtues. As Shakespeare has
it—

> " My love doth so approve him,
>   That e'en his stubbornness, his checks and frowns,
>   Have grace and favor in them."

To make a home you must strengthen the bonds of affection. The Gospel of Christ hallows the affections and sweetens the temper. Come, then, often to the throne of grace, and by prayer enliven your religious sensibilities, which is the very soul of conjugal love and the maturer of those graces that belong to wedlock's string of pearls.

How fitting it was that He who came to restore the Lost Paradise to man should give this significant approval of this sacred bond, and make the Christian home the mightiest instrument in the work of regenerating the human race. The Christian home is the master of life's busy school, the brightest radiance that cheers the darkness of man's earthly condition; it is the guiding star of his good destiny; and the richest earthly prize a man can win is a wife from the Lord.

Christ never meant that home was to be merely a refectory and dormitory, but a place to live. If you would not have your children lost to you in after-life, make home happy to them when they are young. Let it be the place of sparkling joy and innocent amusement, and thus counteract the fashionable tendency of our time to abandon the home and seek pleasure abroad. The reason that so many children make every effort possible to get away from home at night is lack of entertainment at home. Don't reserve all your social charms for friends and strangers abroad, and keep dullness for home consumption.

What might we not hope for this world if we could fill it with happy Christian homes, supported by true men, and presided over by loving women, where every one, young and old, conspired to adorn the home with all the light the mind can yield, and all the love the heart can furnish!

Was Jesus invited to your wedding? Were the nuptial vows sanctified by His presence? Make Him, then, your abiding Guest. Then you will grow in mutual affinity and spiritual assimilation, realizing a happiness in the sacred union which you never dreamed of in your youthful love. Your last days of marriage will be happier than the first, because you lived for each other, and He who was present and sanctified your marriage vows will crown your union with the love that never chills, and keeps on growing until it leaps over the grave and you are caught up to share the unending fellowship of the marriage supper of the Lamb in heaven.

XXXIII.

I AM decidedly opposed to the display of any other flag on our State and municipal buildings than the Stars and Stripes. Imagine Americans in London, Dublin or Rome demanding the display of our flag on the public buildings in those cities on the Fourth of July! When the foreigner becomes an American citizen it is his duty to celebrate our own national holidays. It is perfectly natural to have sympathy for one's native country, and foreigners may with propriety privately celebrate any event that may have been a blessing to the land of their birth, but they have no right to expect the municipal or federal authorities to review their parades or float from the public buildings any other flag than our own flag.

It is deeply to be regretted that many naturalized citizens do not Americanize. On the contrary, they propose to Europeanize America. There is no such thing as "Irish-Americans," "German-Americans" or "Italian-Americans," any more than there are French-Irishmen, Ital-

165

ian-Englishmen or German-Frenchmen. We
must all be Americans. One flag, one country.
There should be no such thing as the "Irish
vote," the "German vote" or "Italian vote,"
for which rascally demagogues of both parties
bid, but only the American vote.

All over our country colonists buy land and
build up States within a State. In the West
I saw little Germanies here, little Scandina-
vias there and little Irelands yonder. Certain
quarters of our city in language, customs and
costumes are essentially foreign. If this in-
sweeping immigration into our land is not
Americanized it will foreignize us. Among
native Americans there is an alarming tendency to depreciate American life. Many
Americans look across the ocean for their example.

I cheerfully admit that thousands upon
thousands of our naturalized citizens are useful and honorable men, an inestimable and in-
dispensable acquisition to our country, and
these adopted citizens of every land and tongue
indorse what I say.

The adopted citizen who is not willing to
adopt these sentiments cannot be a good
American citizen.

XXXIV.

GETTING on in the world does not depend so much upon a man's surroundings as upon himself. God gives to every man wings strong enough to bear him far above his surroundings. If a man does not get up and on he should not blame fate, but himself. The man who gets on in the world cultivates the higher attributes of his manhood, devotes his time to learning how to do better work, which so often insures that prosperity which clamor and complaining never win. The men at the summit fought their way up from the bottom. Columbus was the son of a weaver, Homer of a small farmer, Demosthenes of a cutler, Franklin of a tallow-chandler and soap-boiler, and Shakespeare of a wool-stapler. Robert Burns was a plowman, Napoleon was of an obscure family at Corsica, John Jacob Astor sold apples on the streets of New York, A. T. Stewart swept out his own store, Cornelius Vanderbilt laid the foundation of his vast fortune with fifty dollars given him by his mother, Lincoln was a rail-splitter, Grant was a tanner, and Garfield was a towboy on a canal. Our most successful men began life without a dollar. By hard work and unconquerable perseverance you can rise above the low places of poverty. True, you may never shine in the galaxy of the great ones of this earth, but you may fill your lives and homes with blessings and make the world wiser and better and nobler for your having lived in it. Financial success won at the sacrifice of conscience is the worst kind of a failure. Many crimes have been committed in the name of success. Many men have obtained thousands and millions of dollars by legal or illegal thieving and bought their way into society, who ought to be in the penitentiary. Cash cannot take the place of character. Better to be a man than merely a millionaire. "'Tis only noble to be good." My prescriptions for getting on in the world are simple.

First. Enter into that business for which nature intended you.

Second. Stand on your own legs. The best thing to do is to throw a young man overboard. No man ever drowned who was worth saving.

Third. Work. Ninety per cent. of what men call genius is only a talent for hard work.

The work which most of our successful men do almost staggers belief.

Fourth. Have an aim in life, or your energies will all be wasted and your most industrious days will be recklessly squandered.

Fifth. Inscribe on your banner, "Luck is a fool, Pluck is a hero."

Sixth. Don't try to begin at the top.

Seventh. Watch the littles and you will come out clear.

Eighth. Be punctual. A man who is careless about time is careless about business and cannot be trusted.

Ninth. Let your revenues always exceed your expenditures.

Tenth. Be polite. No policy pays like politeness.

Eleventh. Be upright and down square.

Twelfth. Avoid whiskey and tobacco.

Thirteenth. Be generous. Meanness is a most despicable blemish.

Fourteenth. Don't marry until you can support a wife.

Fifteenth. Make all the money you can honestly, and do good with it while you live.

Be your own executor.

XXXV.

GET-RICH-QUICK SCHEMES.

GET-RICH-QUICK schemes flood our land to-day. Fortunes are offered the people for nothing. The names of scores of men prominent in church and state are published as directors, used as decoy-ducks to draw in the unsuspecting. On every hand are transparent frauds, offers to make you rich for a few dollars, land that will quadruple in a year, and so-called benevolent societies that will in a few years give you one thousand dollars for about three hundred, and meanwhile take care of you in case of sickness. The American people love to be humbugged, and schemes that would pay a legitimate interest often fall through, while the fraud gets the crowd. The only explanation of the prosperity of these transparent frauds is in Carlyle's concise census of the population—"mostly fools."

The misfortune about these schemes is that the poor man is generally the one caught in them. I have known scores of men who by long and severe struggling were enabled at

last to save something. It cost them much
self-denial and care. A hundred plausible
schemes present themselves, all promising a
safe and large return, all demonstrating ten,
twenty or thirty per cent. as certain. The
pulpit speaks of the snares formed to entrap
the wasteful, thoughtless, prodigal man, and
it is high time that it spoke of the schemes
more cunningly devised to entrap the industrious and the thrifty. Multitudes of such persons have had their all swept away, and have
passed their old age in poverty and want, rendered all the more bitter by the reflection that
their suffering was the result of their credu-
lity in trusting to the flattering tales of schem-
ing scoundrels. Know this, that no man will
give you a dollar for fifty cents, unless it is a
counterfeit. Good mines never go begging for
stockholders. A fine spring chicken on your
plate is worth a whole flock of wild geese on
the wing. Leave speculation alone to the men
who can afford to lose the money. Be content
with a small but certain return and run none
of the risks which a great percentage usually
involves. You can tell swindling schemes by
their brilliant colors, plausible appearance and
attractive bait. "All is not gold that glitters,"
and the more glittering there is the less gold
in general.

XXXVI.

WEDDING PRESENTS.

ONE of the most extravagant and hypocritical customs of to-day is the habit of giving wedding presents. Hundreds of invitations are sent to acquaintances, as well as relatives and friends, and their presence is not so much desired as their presents. This is surely a successful way of begging fancy household articles. Many of the presents, being duplicated, are sold or exchanged at a sacrifice for other "more useful" articles. The largeness of a man's heart, the size of his purse and social standing are all determined by the extravagance of the present. Whether it can be afforded or not, people vie with each other, and think they must do as others do, for they would rather be out of the world than out of the fashion. Custom makes cowards of us all. Many wedding presents are never paid for, while others are bought on the instalment plan —dollar down, dollar a week. I have heard many people, and especially poorly salaried society swells, bewail the great expense of this custom. We have frequently heard brides and grooms speak of their presents in a way which showed that the estimates of the various friendships were based on the value of the gift—speaking with delight of the generousness of the one, and condemning the unexpected meanness of the other.

Gifts should be tokens of love and good wishes, and not forced by custom. They should be free-will offerings, and not a universally expected conformity to an arbitrary unwritten law of society. Dare to break away from this hypocrisy.

XXXVII.

POLICE MATRONS.

THE annual report of the Police Department shows that there were 147,634 lodgings in station-houses furnished homeless and friendless persons last year—78,523 to men, and 69,111 to women.

> "Oh, it was pitiful!
> Near a whole city full,
> Home she had none!"

Let us hear no more about "Darkest Africa, and the Way Out" until we have found a way out of "Darkest New York." Think of 82,000 arrests in one year! of which 19,926 were women, 9514 boys under twenty years of age, and 991 of girls under twenty years of age. Most of these arrests were for drunkenness. I would like to know why the poor are always arrested and punished for getting drunk, and the rich never. In other words, it is a crime in New York for a poor man to do what a rich man may do with impunity.

Thousands who apply for lodging in the station-houses are not intoxicated; they are not guilty of any crime; they are only moneyless, homeless, friendless. The men and women, the boys and girls, while not huddled together, are all within hearing and frequently in plain sight of one another; and to compel innocent girls and women to come in contact with the degraded and to be searched by a man certainly tends to make them lose their self-respect, and when a woman once loses that, her case is hopeless indeed. The station-houses of New York need the refining influences which a matron would impart. The objection that the station-house is not a place for a decent woman is the strongest argument possible in favor of the reform. It is unnatural for women to be cared for by persons not of their own sex. Woman knows how to sympathize with woman. In the name of God and decency, I demand that the unfortunate girls and women imprisoned in our station-houses receive the kind treatment which competent matrons alone can give. What is your influence in this matter? We allow men and women to be thrust into cells as if society had a grudge against them, and they in turn have a grudge against society. Give them a hand instead of a heel. Many of them would

leap with joy at the prospect of reformation
if there was a way opened for them into
decency. Many of them are dying for want
of a kind word. Don't blame them. It is not
their fault, but their misfortune. They were
born that way. If our mothers had been blasphemers and our fathers sots, and we had been
rocked in the cradle of vice, we too would sleep
in station-houses instead of palaces. Blood
always tells, especially bad blood. The wrongs
heaped upon the innocent often, and unfortunate always, we should not as Christians be
able to behold without, like our pure and pitiful Master, weeping over them. New York in
the matter of caring for the homeless poor is
a burning disgrace to our boasted Christian
civilization. That old legend of a monster to
satisfy whose appetite a city had every year
to sacrifice a number of its virgins, who, amid
the lamentations of their mothers and the grief
of their kindred, were led away trembling to
his bloody den, is no fable in New York City.
That monster is among us.

Woman, have more sympathy for your fall-
en sisters! Your inhumanity to your own
sex makes countless thousands mourn. Woman, be imbued with the large loving-hearted-
ness of the Gospel, that is unhappy if others
are miserable, that will not eat its own bread

and drink its own cup alone, that is not content to be safe without also saving others.

Parents, guard your children sedulously.
Fold them early. Before the night brings out
the ravenous wolf and the wily fox and the
roaring lion, have all your lambs at home;
prayerfully commit them to the keeping of an
all-present God.

XXXVIII.

WAGES can never be equalized. So long as there are more men who can dig ditches than run a railroad, so long will the railroad president get more wages than the digger of ditches. The ox will always eat more than the rabbit. The premium of higher wages is the great incentive to improvement. Take this away and your workmen are like dried apples on a string, all of one sort and all of one size. Our union-workmen pin each other down, they crush the best laborers down to the level of mediocrity, and cut the heads off their best men.

The capitalists have come up mostly from the multitude. You say they were lucky. I say they were plucky. They got on, but never getting *off*—on sprees, and spending their time in striking and clamoring for higher wages and fewer hours' work per day. They cultivated the higher attributes of manhood, devoted their time to learning how to do better

178

work, which so often insures that prosperity which clamoring, complaining and striking never win.

Let every one start out to be a capitalist himself. When you have saved a dollar from your wages, you have already begun to be a capitalist. Straighten up, reach up, grow up, save up, this is the only way you can get up and crowd off the platform the small faction who abuse their power.

If you want to strike, strike against the drink. Keep it up, and relief will come to the working classes. The late Emperor William and the famous Von Moltke unite in declaring that German beer-drinking is the chief curse of the laboring classes. The late Cardinal Manning of England and the most distinguished judges of the British courts, as well as those men in America who are seeking to ameliorate the condition of the working classes, are agreed that the drink is the worst foe of labor.

The cost of labor to manufacture crude whiskey is about 3½ per cent. on the value of the liquor at the place of manufacture, while, as a distinguished authority has shown, for labor in the aggregate productions of the State there is paid 17.97 per cent. of their value at the place of production. In other words, by buying $100 worth of the aggregate manufactures of our State $14.38 go to labor in their production, while for every $100 spent for liquors to produce them will give only $1.94 to labor. Work will be plenty and wages high by making a demand for useful articles. Let the workingmen spend their money for food, clothing and other necessaries of life with the millions that they now waste for drink, and we will be able to give work to all our unemployed, wages will be high, and labor will no longer be " the slave of capital."

Immigration causes nearly all our labor troubles. Within the last three years we admitted into the American labor market 427,000 Hungarians, Italians and Poles. What can our laboring men gain by striking for higher wages when every steamship brings hundreds of starving immigrants who are glad to get work at any price? We pay enormous sums for the ostensible purpose of protecting the American workman, yet everywhere the pauper laborer of Europe swarms in his path and competes with native industry by offering to do work for half the price paid the American laborer. Thousands came under service to contractors who sell their labor. You can buy one or a thousand laborers from the Italian padrones in this city.

Our present system of importing labor free means to degrade the American workman to a level with the pauper laborers of Europe. Neither high protection nor free trade makes wages so high as scarcity of hands. If we could stop immigration for twenty years, high tariff, low tariff or no tariff, the American workman would enjoy prosperity never dreamt of.

XXXIX

TOBACCO THE FOE OF WOMAN.

TOBACCO is the foe of woman. It withdraws man from her society—banishing him for hours from the civilizing sex. Thackeray says: "The fact is, the cigar is a rival to the ladies, and their conqueror, too." The Turks shut the women in; we shut them out. Many physicians regard much of the invalidism of women due to the poisoned atmosphere around them by the smoking members of their household. Many a woman have I heard speak feelingly of the clean atmosphere of houses untainted with tobacco. How many a delicate woman is affected by the least tobacco breath, and then think of her yoked to one who uses the weed perpetually. How much of life's pleasure is spoiled by this ever-following foe. Everywhere you go is splashed the disgusting fluid. The passages between the seats of our railroad and street-cars are, as a rule, in such a foul condition that no lady can walk with safety or comfort from the seat to the door. There's little use in carefully holding up your dresses and looking warily from place to place. You might as well take the first seat that comes. No wonder the women lose their temper almost every time they travel in our cars. Just look at the men: they chew and spit, they read and spit, they talk and spit, they laugh and spit, and some swear and spit.

"Is smoking offensive to you?" What is the woman to do? If she tells the truth, the gentleman will not lay down his cigar, but retreat to enjoy his smoke elsewhere, and the woman feels that she has been guilty of rudeness. If smoking is not an annoyance, how do you interpret the conspicuous posters everywhere warning against it where the ladies gather? It is from a loving readiness on the part of the women to sacrifice their own comfort to the gratification of their dear ones that they submit to this tyrant, and in this, together with lack of information on the subject, we find an explanation of its almost universal sway.

In a certain town a number of young women formed a "*No society*"; that is, they would have no intercourse with any young man who used tobacco, or who was not strictly temper-

ate. At first the young men made themselves
merry over this, declaring that they could
stand out as long as the girls. But these girls
quietly held to their resolves; and gradually
one young man after another broke from his
obnoxious habit, till tobacco and the wine-cup
were banished from the circle.

If all the women had the courage of their
convictions, gentlemen, your time would be
short. Instead of, for policy's sake, condoning
an offense which puts in jeopardy your health,
which tends to lower æsthetic tone, and involves a train of miseries, women, speak out
boldly, and exert your influence, singly and
collectively, against tobacco, and you cannot
fail to batter down this ugly brown idol past
all resurrection.

In true gallantry the American is ahead of
all the world. Could we secure this most-
devoutly-wished-for reform, it would add the
finishing touch, and exalt this same American
into the ideal gentleman.

XL.

OUR WHITE SLAVES.

" So I returned, and considered all the oppressions that are done under the sun : and behold the tears of such as were oppressed, and they had no comforter ; and on the side of their oppressors there was power ; but they had no comforter."—
ECCLESIASTES iv. 1.

I HAD read so much in the daily papers about the "sweating" system on the East Side in New York City, that I determined to see for myself if these things were true. In company with a labor agitator and a newspaper man, both of whom thoroughly understood the system, I started on my trip of investigation. The reporter and the writer were introduced to the contractors by the labor man as factory inspectors. That the contractors did not know that we were not factory inspectors proves that the inspectors do not inspect.

I saw human beings almost piled upon one another and buried out of sight in masses of materials, which smelt as powerfully and as poisonously as the wretched toilers themselves.

The factories are out-of-the-way places, bed-rooms, rear lofts, and subcellars. In many instances the employed live, work and sleep huddled together in these shops.

Ten years ago there were only 10 sweaters' shops in New York, but now there are 750, and work that brought $5 and $6 then realizes only $1.50 now. Hardly any one will believe the truth unless he has seen it. If the philan-thropic people of this city could visit these places, they would soon band together for their abolition. These people have suffered so long, they have borne so much, that the wonder is that they are as moderate as they are. Can you imagine the feelings of a man who has to work eighty to ninety hours a week for $4? There are 16,000 operators in garments for women and operators in cloaks for children; there are 24,000 clothing-makers. There are twelve Hebrew papers published for this pop-ulation. Some of these papers are socialistic. These men look about them, and so great are the contrasts in society that their faith is shaken.

The contractors are generally men from the ranks of the immigrants. They hire a loft, or two bare rooms, for about $18 per month, get a pile of clothing from the manufacturer, who tells the price he will pay for each completed garment, and then they hire their hands. The market is overstocked with labor, and there are hundreds ready to take the place at any price. Nowadays the cloak is the product of fifteen poor refugees (each making a part), huddled together under the foulest physical conditions, working from fifteen to eighteen hours a day as fast as their feet and hands can go. I don't think that I found among the sweaters' employees an operator forty years old. They die or are struck down by disease long before that time.

But you must now take a trip with me to a sweater's den on Mulberry Street. The entrance is narrow and squalid, up three flights of ladder-like stairs, through a door, rickety and grimy. Taking us for officers, we were hailed, " Vat you vanta ? " " These gentlemen," said our spokesman, " are factory inspectors. You must answer any question they put to you." We are in a small, poorly ventilated loft. The windows are black with dirt from poisonous fluff from garments. The air is stifling, the ceiling low, the heat intense. To work as prisoners for crime would have been a respite for these sad-faced foreigners.

The following figures were obtained from the " boss sweaters " themselves and are therefore reliable :

For making overcoats....................	$0 75 to	$2 50
For making business coats	32 to	1 50
For making trousers....................	25 to	75
For making vests (per doz.).............	1 00 to	3 00
For making knee-pants (per doz.)........	50 to	75
For making calico shirts (per doz.).......	30 to	45

A large percentage is taken from this list of prices by the boss sweater as his profit, and after deducting the cost of carting, which the workman pays, it can easily be imagined how hard and long men and women must labor to obtain the ordinary necessities of life. For knee-pants, for which the "boss" gets sixty-five cents a dozen from the manufacturer, the sweated get only thirty-five cents. Almost everywhere we found children hard at work. As I thought of the joyous childhood up-town filled with innocent pleasure, and then contemplated these slaves of the needle working from twelve to eighteen hours a day in a miserable hovel for $1.50 to $4 a week, and then to sleep in a room with a dozen men and women, herding together like cattle, I said, What a subject for tears of compassion! This injustice, oppression and suffering! What a theme for the reformer or the novelist! These inhumanly long hours! These starvation wages!

We went through the markets as Commissioners of the Board of Health. Hester Street was blockaded by the peddlers. "Meat, four cents a pound"; "Apples, five for a cent"; "Fish, four cents a pound," were common signs. Here are dozens of restaurants where a dinner with fish and two glasses of beer is to be had for thirteen cents. The quality of this food is better imagined than described. And the result of eating such food is a mind and body subject to an insatiable thirst for drink, and this fact makes drunkards of many who would otherwise be sober people. There is an intimate relation between the body and soul, and this question of better food for the poor is a moral question. The chief cause of poverty is drink, but the chief cause of the craving for drink among the poor is lack of healthy food. Napoleon once said, "The soldier has his heart in his abdomen;" and Von Moltke gave emphasis to the moral force of good food when he said, "In a campaign no food is costly except that which is bad."

Philanthropists, investigate this system which grinds human creatures' lives into dust! How long shall this injustice continue upon these helpless foreigners, giving the lie to American freedom? Out upon this corrupting farce! Down with this entirely abominable system! Let our Factory Law be so amended as to strike directly at tenement factories, and make a new law forbidding the toiler to labor fifteen to eighteen hours a day for the wages of a day, and a blow will be struck at this system from which it will never recover. Our duty is solemn and pressing. The words of the late Cardinal Manning to the Committee of the House of Lords, when investigating the sweaters' dens in London, are applicable here to-day: " If the hours of labor, resulting from an unregulated sale of a man's strength and skill, shall lead to the destruction of domestic life, to the neglect of children, to turning wives and mothers into living machines, and fathers and husbands into creatures of burden, the domestic life exists no longer, and we dare not go on in this path."

XLI.

THE POOR CHILDREN OF NEW YORK.

"Famine is in their cheeks;
Need and oppression staring in their looks,
Contempt and beggary hang upon their backs."

This is not only poetry, but the fact of thousands of children in New York City; yet the merry laugh, the hearty shout and screams of delight, tell that God made childhood to be happy, and how even misery will forget itself in the buoyancy of youth. Beneath the shaggy bushes of hair and faces pinched with want, behold a sharp intelligence beyond their years. These little street arabs are already masters of imposture, lying, begging, stealing. No blame to them, but much blame to those who neglected them—they had otherwise perished. There is so much misery among New York's poor that we have almost ceased to be astonished at any amount of misery suffered.

We have splendid hospitals and schools where thousands of children are fed and clothed and educated, but what provision have we made for these children of crime, misery and misfortune? None! I doubt if any pulpit in this city ever thought that this question was important enough for discussion. These homeless and godless poor little ones that we are neglecting into vice and starving into crime should through Christian charity be pressing the narrow path of life. Those cursing little lips should be singing the praises of God. The Spartans who threw their sickly children to the wild beasts were merciful compared with that indifference which in our city gives up the destitute children to be eaten up by their own depravities.

Why are these thousands of children upon the streets and not at school? Listen to the reply: "No room!" If there were room the reply would be of the parents, "Can't afford to keep them there." They must beg, and next thing to begging is stealing. They are cast into prison; the jail brand is on their brow; self-respect is lost; they descend from step to step till they end their unhappy careers, the victims of a poverty for which they were not to blame, and for a neglect on the part of a Christian public for which a righteous God will one day call them to judgment.

If these poor children cannot attend school unless they starve, feed them in order to educate them. Food is a powerful magnet to draw a hungry child to school. Don't mock with books a child who wants for bread. Prevention of crime is cheaper than its punishment. There is only one way of securing the amelioration of these outcast children, and that is by making their maintenance a bridge and a stepping-stone to their education. " When thy father and thy mother forsake thee, the Lord will take thee up." How ? By putting it into the hearts of his people to do a father's and a mother's part to those who are fatherless and motherless, or to those still more unhappy children who have parents but would be better off if they had none.

Let there be schools for all the children ; make education compulsory, and provide the means for the compulsion. Let the schoolhouses be open evenings, and filled with books, papers and games. Put your hands on the hearts of the little ones, surround them with benign and holy influences, and these children, though their knees are now out, their elbows out, their toes out, and their souls Christless, will grow up to be men of might and men of God.

XLII.

DR. BRIGGS'S acquittal is a vindication of historic Presbyterianism. John Calvin, who so clearly expounded and so perfectly systematized the Pauline theology as to connect with it his illustrious name, made Geneva the capital of European reform and the cradle of civil and religious liberty. The historic distinction of the Presbyterian Church is its intimate connection with civil and religious liberty. Tyrants and despots, whether civil or religious, have always hated Presbyterianism. King James said at the Hampton Court Conference, "Ye are aiming at a Scots Presbytery, which agrees with monarchy as well as God and the devil." To the Calvinistic Melville he said, "There will be no quiet in this country till half a dozen of ye be hanged or banished." "Tush, sir!" replied Melville, "threaten your courtiers in that manner; but, God be glorified, it will not be in your power to hang or exile his truth." "The doctrine" (Presbyterianism), said Charles I., "is anti-monarchical—no bishop, no king." *The Westminster Review*, which certainly has no love for Presbyterianism, says, "Calvin sowed the seeds of liberty in Europe." Again it says, "Calvinism saved Europe." Bossuet, the Roman Catholic historian, speaking of the General Synod of France in 1559, says: "A great social revolution has been effected. Within the center of the French monarchy Calvin and his disciples established a spiritual republic," and out of it came the French Republic. Macaulay has shown that the great revolution of 1688, which gave liberty to England, was purchased by the labors and the blood of the Presbyterians of Scotland. Froude admits that the Scotch owe their national existence to the teachings of John Knox. The same author says, "Calvin has done more for constitutional liberty than any one man."

The Presbyterian Synod in Philadelphia in 1775 was the first religious body to declare for American independence, and to counsel and encourage the people who were then about taking up arms. The "Mecklenburg Declaration," proclaimed by the Scotch-Irish Presbyterians of North Carolina, May 20, 1775, and written by a Presbyterian elder and Princeton graduate, Brevard, is so similar in sentiment and expression that Jefferson must have borrowed from Brevard, who wrote a year before Jefferson wrote.

Charles Inglis, rector of Trinity Church, in reporting to " The Church Missionary Society " at London, says that " without one exception all our clergy are on the side of the crown, and after strict inquiry I do not know one of the Presbyterian clergy who does not, by every effort in his power, promote all the measures of Congress, however extravagant."

Chief-justice Tilghman says that " the framers of the Constitution of the United States borrowed very much of the form of our republic from that form of Presbyterian government developed in the constitution of the Presbyterian Church in Scotland." Bancroft says, " He that will not honor and respect the influence of John Calvin knows but little of the origin of American liberty." A church so pre-eminently identified with civil and religious liberty would blot her history by now turning a man out of her communion for saying things which don't exactly square with the Confession of Faith—a confession that originated more than two hundred years ago in a divided assembly, and which articles were even then carried by a bare majority, with strong protest against them.

There are many intellectual roads to heaven. The only intolerance we should tolerate is intolerance of evil, and the only narrowness we should know is narrowness at the point of character. Let our brethren henceforth keep their differences to themselves, and not give the enemy occasion to blaspheme. As John Calvin said, " Let us have no discord on account of our differences, but let us march in one solid column under the banners of the Captain of our salvation, and with undivided counsels pour the legions of the cross upon the territories of darkness and death."

XLIII.

THE restoration of Dr. McGlynn to his priestly functions, unconditionally and without apology, in spite of his defiant attitude and unrelenting criticisms of persons and policies in the church ever since his excommunication, is the most significant ecclesiastical event of a generation. It is one of the grandest triumphs of the century for Americanism. The ultramontane interpretation of the power of the Pope to lord over the consciences of men has received a blow from which it may never recover. It is as inconsistent with our American liberties to yield allegiance to the Pope as to the Czar. The American Catholic who believes that he must unresistingly and uninquiringly obey the Pope or offend God is happily becoming the exception and not the rule, especially among representative laymen.

There are Catholics in this country no more American than they were before they left Europe, and it is gratifying that they have

198

received no comfort from the Pope's representative. The Catholic Church is not only the greatest police force in America, but one of the greatest moral forces tending to the weal or woe of the Republic as it adapts itself or not to the spirit of our American institutions.

The Catholic Church in America is more American than Roman, and the McGlynn incident and Father Corrigan's triumph mean that the church will grow into closer touch with American life and institution; and policy rather than principle forces the church to adjust herself to the sacred rights of free thought, free speech and free action, the immortal principles of Americanism.

Papal interference with politics reduced Italy to a hand-organ and a monkey, Spain to beggary, Ireland to exile, and American Catholics will profit by their example. But the church seems to have quit politics. She is minding her own business, and the liberalizing of the Catholic Church will win to her the unchurched masses, especially if the church will seek the solution of those social problems which have alienated the masses from the church. Such old words with new meanings, as altruism, anarchy, communism, nihilism, socialism and the like, show that sociology is the great problem of the day—the problem which Protestant ministers ignore with owl-like stupidity, while they are spending their time in spinning theological cobwebs and building speculative castles in the air.

Dr. McGlynn's restoration is a victory for our public schools—one of the corner-stones of our government. The American Catholics read with profit the course the church pursued as to popular education where she had undisputed sway. In Italy 73 per cent. of the population are illiterate, Spain 80 per cent., and Mexico 93 per cent. The American Catholics no longer believe in the proverb that "ignorance is the mother of devotion." The church is not only opening schools of her own, but many parents send their children to the public schools, and some of her archbishops and priests are eloquent defenders of what we may proudly call the glory of our Republic. Glad beyond telling am I that the Pope has at last recognized that it would be a vital blunder to continue in the organized hostility to the public school which the radical ecclesiastics have heretofore pursued, and it is to be hoped, as a result of his wise counsels, that there will be an end to this exasperating controversy.

We are engaged, as Bacon said, in "the heroic work of building a nation," and whether Catholics or Protestants, let us remember that

we are Americans first, and no despotism shall
be introduced here, whether in politics or religion. Let us be free men in politics and religion—free to read, to think, to act, and to
control our own affairs. Let us adopt the
American plan of liberty, discard the timorous
fear of error, and trust to the mighty power
of truth. Cast off slavery; every man go to
the fountains of truth and taste and judge for
himself. Methinks I see the dawn of a coming
day when Catholic and Protestant, Jew and
Gentile, will unite as American citizens in
maintaining our public schools and all our
public institutions on a public basis.

XLIV.

Municipal Corruption.

THE sword of Justice, which should be a terror to evil-doers, rusts in its sheath. The machinery of our law lies in City Hall in polished inactivity. Vice is allowed to so parade our streets as to interfere with the freedom of the virtuous, and establishes itself under police protection in decent communities, and by creating the worst kind of nuisances destroys the property of a neighborhood, and evil-doers are protected at the expense of the good.

Clean Government.

The only government decent men ought to tolerate is honorable government. The man who neglects to take sides on this question of clean government for our city makes choice of ease and quiet at the expense of purity and power. If you want a clean city, vote to get the government into clean hands. The great failure of our Republican system is the failure to give our cities decent government. We will have good government when good citizens come up to the mark of good citizenship, when men vote as they pray. I have the profoundest contempt for the man who prays like an angel and votes like the devil.

Treating.

Treating is the cause of more than one half of our drunkenness. America is the only country where this foolish and expensive show of hospitality is recognized. Many young men are established in intemperance because they feel themselves bound by a law of reciprocal generosity to treat.

Wanted—Old-fashioned Mothers.

What America wants now is about one million old-fashioned mothers who shall realize that the grandest and mightiest institution on earth is the home. The duties of motherhood are nowadays considered too commonplace tasks for women. So when a child is born a nurse is hired, who for a compensation agrees to take charge of the little immortal. She hands over to a mere hireling the soul-mothering which God has intrusted to the mother. The little one draws into its inner being the life of this uncultured soul. The young mother is free to keep on in the old gay life, free to pet pugs, to dress and drive, to enjoy balls and operas, to pay gossip visits and attend "teas," which Oliver Wendell Holmes well describes as "a giggle, gabble, gobble and git," while she discharges her trust for an immortal life by proxy. Oh, that God would give every mother a vision of the glory and splendor of the work that is given to her when a babe is placed on her bosom to be nursed and trained!

The Bible in the Public Schools.

If this generation gets the Bible out of our public schools, putting the ban of sectarian ignominy upon it, another generation will not be likely to restore it. The Bible is the property of mankind and therefore not a sectarian book. The Bible is older than any sect in the world. Our English translation of the Bible is no more a Protestant book than the Bible itself in the original is a Protestant book.

You are bound to suppose as much conscience on the Protestant as on the Catholic side. Shall the conscience of the smaller number bind that of the larger? If conscience is to be respected, then the greater amount of conscience is to be respected rather than the smaller. If it be found on the side of the

Bible it ought to prevail in the right to have the Bible. Our Catholic brethren tell us that they have a right to demand of the government a school according to their principles because they pay their taxes. Then the majority of tax-payers have the same right to demand a school according to their principles.

Divorce the public schools from the Bible, and you divorce them from the respect and patronage of Christians, and so divorced they cannot stand.

Bribery.

Political jobbery and corruption are fast undermining the efficiency of our free institutions and debasing the standard of public virtue. Politics has become a mere race for pelf and self. Patriotism is abandoned and principle is almost a forgotten virtue. It is therefore in place for the pulpit to call the attention of candidates and politicians to this evil. Our State law makes it unlawful, directly or indirectly, to pay, lend or offer money or any other thing to a voter to induce him to vote or to refrain from voting. He who by false registration, colonizing, intimidation, buying or selling votes, or in any way whatever, interferes with the American ballot is unworthy of citizenship. If ever a man is justified in thrashing another, it is to thrash him whose soul is so dead to honor as to trade in American citizenship.

Athletics gone Mad.

Pascal declared that " disease is the natural state of Christians," and many persons still think that asceticism is righteousness and dyspepsia godliness. The enthusiasm for athletics to-day is a reaction from the unwise indifference of the past. The Israelites worshiped a calf of gold. The Americans bow down before a calf of flesh. Athletics is the principal topic of conversation. The boxing-glove may yet be woven upon our flag. Colleges take their grades according to their records in sports. Noses are smashed and fingers broken to the delight of assembled thousands. We squander more money on theaters, baseball, horse races, prize fights and clubs than we do on food and clothes, education and religion. The major part of our sports totally unfits those who take part in them for the active work of life. Our sporting craze is the indirect cause of nine-tenths of our financial crimes.

This sporting tendency is, indeed, our national sin. The chief cause of the downfall of Rome was the sporting habits of the people. With the brute fight before us at New Orleans, let the American pulpit say no more about the gladiatorial shows of heathen Rome or the bull fights of Spain or Mexico. All decent people rejoiced in the New Orleans result, because they had contempt for the strong brute who was vanquished. Strength without character is revolting.

Athletics is desirable. I hope its result will be a finer race. But if you cultivate the physical exclusively you have a savage. Brawn and brain, muscle and manhood, strength and character, must be blended to make a strong man. George MacDonald gives sound advice to those who have the upbringing of children when he counsels them to treat them " as souls having bodies rather than as bodies having souls." To depreciate the body to the exaltation of the soul, as though it were at best an encumbrance, is without support in the Bible.

Immigration and Labor.

When employment can be had at all in the Old World, laborers receive the following wages, namely:

In India (300,000,000 people)......... but 10 cents per day.
In Russia (100,000,000 people).... but 25 to 50 cents per day.
In Sweden...................... but 26 to 52 cents per day.
In Denmark...................... but 26 to 50 cents per day.
In Norway..................... but 26 to 52 cents per day.

In Finland....................	but 26 to	52 cents per day.
In Spain	but 40 to	60 cents per day.
In Italy.....................	but 50 to	90 cents per day.
In France....................	but 50 to	90 cents per day.
In Germany	but 45 to	75 cents per day.
In Austro-Hungary............	but 45 to	75 cents per day.
In Great Britain.............	but 62 to	$1.08 cents per day.

A careful examination of the prices current
in England and the United States proves that
a dollar will buy more tea, coffee, lamp-oil,
flour, meat, butter, bread, sugar and potatoes
in the United States than it will in England
or any other part of Europe, while a single
pound of beef in many of these foreign countries costs as much as a day's wages will buy.

Through our unrestricted immigration all
the world competes with our workmen in our
own country. The thousands upon thousands
that are idle in every land in the Old World
come to America to the detriment of our own
workmen. If immigration continues, how
long will the American workman be the best
housed, the best fed and the best paid workman in the world? The immigrant of to-day
not only lowers the dignity and debases the
blood of labor, but is driving the American
laborer from our mills, shops and markets,
and if the present tide continues for twenty
years we will see many of our best citizens
going from the United States and the scum

of Europe will take their places. The time was when the immigrants growing dissatisfied with a manufacturing center could emigrate to the West and take up land on which to build a home. That day exists only in history. Our government has squandered the good land with a lavish hand, and though there are millions of acres still unoccupied it must be remembered that it is land so poor that you could not raise a row on it.

Europe's own sins produced the scabs on its body politic, and they have long enough escaped punishment by sending their paupers and criminals to America. Let these degraded hordes of unenlightened nations remain where they are until they have shaken the foundations of every monarchy across the water, rather than see the only home in which freedom has a foothold vanish from the face of the political world.

Home Rule for America.

The total population in New York State in 1891 numbered 5,997,853. This number was composed of 2,594,708 persons born of native parents (including the colored population of 73,901), 1,837,453 born of foreign parents and 1,565,692 foreigners, exceeding those born of native parents by 808,437. These millions concentrate largely in Albany, Kings, Erie, Rensselaer and New York counties. These counties are entitled to nearly one-half the members of the legislature. In Rensselaer County the foreigners have a majority of 13,-551; in Albany County the native-born population is in a minority of 37,315; in Erie the whites of native parentage are in a minority of 148,887; in Kings 360,921; and in New York the foreign element has the immense majority of 948,653. When we remember how small pluralities determine our State and Presidential elections, it can be easily seen how small a figure the American cuts in the government of his native land. Home rule for America may yet become an issue in our politics.

Should immigration continue for ten years more to the extent of ten years past, the foreign element will have an overwhelming preponderance in the Northern States. No thoughtful well-wisher of the State or of the Republic can regard this tendency without apprehension. Has not America become too much of a "free" country?

People's Clubs.

Under existing social conditions the saloon supplies a popular want, and the masses will stand by the saloon, though it is their worst enemy, until they are provided with some counter attraction. The establishment of people's clubs, saloons without liquor, after the fashion of the coffee-houses in England, or the People's Palace in London, would, in a measure at least, counteract the saloon influence.

Men want to go somewhere when the day's work is done. The saloons are attractive, many of them being invested with all the attractions which the wealth of brewers, who own most of them, can give them. The church must establish houses that beat the public-houses. Marble and glass, drapery and pictures, music and games are not the devil's any more than they are ours. The people will have some retreat besides the boarding-house or tenement dens, and if the church won't furnish them a place to go to, the devil will.

Never Judge by Appearances.

Never before was our society so much of a "Vanity Fair." Every frog seems ambitious to swell himself to the dimensions of an ox. No wonder the frog bursts.

Trying to be somebody when you are nobody is up-hill work. Leading a $10,000 existence on a $5000 salary is a fruitful source of financial crime and moral suicide. A few can live in princely style, but the many must live moderately, or get money by dishonorable methods.

Gaudy parlors and empty kitchens! Wives and daughters covered with costly ornaments (more diamonds (?) are worn to-day than all the diamond fields of the world could produce in a century), living in fine houses on fashionable streets, while husbands and fathers are driven to distraction, many of them to prison, to obtain the gold to maintain the glitter. What shifts, what sleepless nights, simply that they may move in fashionable society and extract compliments and flatteries which are as hollow as they are insincere. The gaudy, tinselled side out, rags and starvation within! Misery magnificent! Poverty gilded! Smiles abroad, tears at home!

> "Appearances deceive,
> And this one maxim is a standing rule,
> Men are not what they seem."

Tobacco and Christianity.

In 1499 Columbus, lying off Cuba, sent two men ashore, and they came back with the smoker's pedigree, to wit: *The naked savages twist leaves together, light one end at the fire, and smoke like devils.*

The annual production of tobacco throughout the world is estimated at four billions of pounds. This mass, if transformed into rolled tobacco two inches in diameter, would coil around the world sixty times. The yearly expense of this poisonous growth, put into marketable shape, reaches one thousand millions of dollars. This would build a hundred thousand churches, each costing ten thousand dollars; or it would employ a million of preachers at one thousand dollars.

In the United States 638,841 acres of land are devoted to this weed. The number of pounds raised is nearly five hundred millions, and four thousand millions of cigars and seven hundred millions of cigarettes are manufactured annually in our country. Our annual tobacco bill is over $250,000,000, while the total contributions of all the churches in America, for all causes, do not exceed $77,-000,000. Thousands of our church members spend ten dollars for tobacco to one dollar for church and charity. Fifty men in most of our churches spend more in the aggregate every year for tobacco than the whole church gives for charity. What records to appear on the heavenly ledger! The money which the Christians of New York spend for tobacco would handsomely shelter, feed, educate and Christianize our suffering poor. What is your Christian influence in this respect? Don't you think it would be better for you to practice a little self-denial?

One reason why this habit goes on from destruction to destruction is because so many ministers of the gospel are worshiping this ugly brown idol. I have seen spittoons in pulpits. The Levites were required to be thoroughly clean and pure. The rules of Buddha strictly interdict the use of tobacco. Shall we allow in our pulpits that which would not be tolerated in Jewish, Chinese or Indian temples? I know ministers who smoke until their breath is as rank as that of a foul beast and their clothes have the odor of the sewer. They smoke themselves into *parsonitis*, commonly called bronchitis; they smoke until their nerves are shattered and their brains begin to soften, and their congregations must send them off to recuperate from their exhausting religious duties.

Oh, for a breath from the heights of heaven that shall drive out this foul odor from the church and cleanse every Christian of this filthy habit!

Homicide and Suicide.

Our land is red with the blood of the homicide and suicide. It is estimated that sixty-one persons die daily from premeditated violence. Have you seen a paper in the last ten years that did not announce a murder or a passage out of life by one's own behest?

Homicides predominate in the South, while suicides are most frequent in the North. I account for this because one-third of the male population in the South carry concealed weapons, and because of a false standard of personal honor. A Tennessee judge says, "More than half the homicides which occur grow out of the debased practice of carrying on the person concealed weapons."

In the North there are more suicides among women than in the South. The Southern woman has less marital misery. Divorces in the South are few. In Chicago alone there are more applications for divorces in one year than among the entire white native population in all the Southern States east of the Mississippi. Easy divorce causes the alarming increase of female suicides.

A prolific source of suicidism is in the fact that we lay too high a value on success in life. Hence, if men fail to get rich, or are exposed, suicide is often the resort. The coward sneaks to death, the brave live on. He is not valiant that dares die, but that boldly bears calamity. Win success if you can, but don't blow your brains out because you fail. God, in the Bible, looks upon suicide as a crime, and that man who, in the use of his reason, dies by his own act goes straight into perdition. All the good men and women of the Bible left their earthly terminus to God. If any man had a right to commit suicide Job had. All his property gone, all his children slain, and from the crown of his head to the soles of his feet covered with boils, pestered by his wife, who was the worst boil he had—unmindful of all the comfortless talk about him, he sat down on a heap of ashes, with only a broken piece of pottery in the surgery of his wounds, yet crying in triumph, "All the days of my appointed time will I wait till my change come."

You may sometimes have reasons for wanting to get to that sorrowless world where there are no notes to pay, no sickness to torment, no wolf of want to keep away from the door of the house you love, but where there will be everything grand and without cost, but you will never get there by hurling yourself out of life. God wants you to live here until you are fit to live somewhere else.

Don't jump out of the frying-pan into the fire!

www.ingramcontent.com/pod-product-compliance
Lightning Source LLC
Chambersburg PA
CBHW020604030726
47497CB00007B/2075